WATCH
THE
LAMB

WATCH THE LAMB

A Fresh Look at Jesus

While this book has been written for group studies, it is also intended for your personal enjoyment.

TERRY BELL

Christian Communications
P.O. Box 150
Nashville, Tennessee 37202

Christian Communications is a division of the Gospel Advocate Co., P. O. Box 150, Nashville, TN 37202.

ISBN 0-89225-344-4

Second Printing, 1992

Foreword

by John C. Stevens

Chancellor, Abilene Christian University

This is a great book! These chapters were originally prepared as sermons at the Hillcrest Church of Christ in Abilene, Texas. So many people have requested tapes and copies that it was thought advisable to publish this book of thirteen lessons for study and meditation.

It has been my privilege to hear Dr. Terry Bell's preaching for the past seven years, and therefore I have heard him preach most of the sermons contained in this book.

A Terry Bell sermon is always well prepared. He does not go into the pulpit (or rather, stand in front of it as he usually does) to make impromptu comments. Every sermon has been diligently studied and written out word for word. Now, although he writes his sermons, he does not read them. In fact, he does not even have notes to consult, at least so far as one can see. But back of his presentation one can always tell that there have been hours of painstaking preparation. He knows what he wants to say and he says it very well.

Furthermore, Terry's sermons always show evidence of prayer. He prays, believes in prayer, preaches much about prayer. His sermons are enriched thereby.

The sermons are Biblical. He always begins by asking the congregation to open Bibles and read with him.

His lessons have a purpose. He does not preach and he does not write just to fulfill a duty. His purpose is to draw men and women to Christ and to build their faith.

I hope the readers of this book will find as much food for thought and for the soul as I have found. I commend it wholeheartedly.

For Jan
my constant inspiration

Contents

1   Watch The Lamb!   3

2   When The Answers Don't Come 15

3   How To Enjoy The Party 27

4   God Is A Gambler 39

5   Just Say The Word 49

6   When God Is Silent 61

7   When God Is Still 73

8   How Should I Act Anyway? 83

9   Following Through When The Going
      Gets Rough 95

10   When Jesus Went To A Homecoming 109

11   Making Religion Personal 121

12   The First Sunday Night Church Service 131

13   Where Do We Go From Here? 141

JOHN 1:29-36

The next day John saw Jesus coming toward him and said, "Look, the Lamb of God, who takes away the sin of the world! This is the one I meant when I said, 'A man who comes after me has surpassed me because he was before me.' I myself did not know him, but the reason I came baptizing with water was that he might be revealed to Israel."

Then John gave this testimony: "I saw the Spirit come down from heaven as a dove and remain on him. I would not have known him, except that the one who sent me to baptize with water told me, 'The man on whom you see the Spirit come down and remain is he who will baptize with the Holy Spirit.' I have seen and I testify that this is the Son of God."

The next day John was there again with two of his disciples. When he saw Jesus passing by, he said, "Look, the Lamb of God!"

1

Watch The Lamb!

John 1:29-36

For four hundred years Israel had had no prophet. By now the prophets were all part of a proud national history, their names known to every devout Jew. Moses, Samuel, Isaiah, Jeremiah—they were not only religious celebrities, but national heroes. They were also every Israelite's assurance that Israel was still the chosen nation of God; that God had not left; that He had not wearied of the constant lack of loyalty and devotion.

But four hundred years had passed since the prophetic voice had been heard in Israel. Once again, however, the air was charged with new excitement.

Out in the wilderness, a new prophet came forth, wearing camel skin and eating locusts and wild honey. In the finest tradition of the prophets, he preached coming judgment and the need for repentance. People everywhere flocked to hear him preach. Thousands listened and were baptized by him or his disciples. Somehow they knew . . . God had come back . . . the silence was broken . . . the prophet had returned.

The tone of his preaching was sharp and disquieting, like pouring salt into a fresh wound. Not everyone could take it. Enemies challenged him, but he never blinked an eye. He knew who he was and whose he was; the stern message continued to pour forth with hot passion.

He commanded repentance. No doubt he attacked their favorite sins, becoming downright personal and sometimes cruel. He called them a brood of vipers and refused them baptism unless they showed evidence of

---

ISAAC MAY HAVE FORGOTTEN HIS SIXTH BIRTHDAY, OR HIS FIRST HUNTING TRIP, OR HIS FIRST ROMANCE, BUT I GUARANTEE YOU ONE THING: HE NEVER FORGOT THE DAY THAT GOD PROVIDED A SUBSTITUTE FOR HIS SACRIFICE.

---

repentance. He warned that the ax was at the root and unless they changed they would be cut down and burned. His language was as hot as the desert from which he came.

He was a different kind of prophet from what we might expect the announcer of the Messiah to be. He was in line with the heritage of the ancient prophets: "Judgment is coming unless you repent." His message echoed those of Elijah, Isaiah, and Ezekiel. Historically and culturally the people identified with him.

No church today would hire John the Baptist. He had not been to the right schools; his language was abrasive as sandpaper, and we would be preoccupied with an unbalanced gospel: A gospel without judgment! We would have settled for a gospel that allowed us to be at ease with our favorite sins. What would John the Baptist say today?

In contrast to all his usual sternness, John's first words when he saw Jesus were absolutely amazing: "Look, the Lamb of God . . ." (v. 29).

How different from the harshness of his earlier sermons. Nothing about snakes; nothing about fire; nothing about an ax at the root. Now he was talking about a lamb—gentle, meek, and innocent. "Look, the Lamb of God, who takes away the sin of the world!" (v. 29).

Like a good preacher, he points out with clarity the sin, and then he pointed out the Sinbearer. And he called Him the "Lamb of God."

THE LAMB AS A SYMBOL

The symbol of the lamb had a rich history in Israel. The very first book of the law introduced the "lamb." Every good Jew knew the story of father Abraham, his son Isaac . . . and the lamb.

The drama unfolds for us in Genesis 22:2. "Then God said, Take your son, your only son Isaac, whom you love, and go to the region of Moriah. Sacrifice him there as a burnt offering . . ." Surely, every Jewish father felt the agony of the thought; surely, every Jewish son saw the flash of the knife.

When they got to the mountain the boy asked the right question. He saw the wood, the knife, and the fire. But where is the lamb? Beyond the picture of Abraham's devotion to God is a story more personal to each of us.

Where is the lamb? God has required a sacrifice from the beginning; a blood sacrifice! From the time of Abel to the time of Abraham to the time of America, God has required a blood sacrifice. Where is the lamb? And if there is no lamb, the alternatives are unthinkable!

Suddenly it dawned on Isaac: Since no lamb was to be found, he would be the one to be sacrificed. I can't imagine the scene. The tears, the deep guttural sobbing, the nausea, the ache in the throat. Every fatherly instinct rebelled against the act. Abraham tied the terrified, trembling boy, the son, and took the knife . . .

Where is the lamb? With aching wrists and knuckles, with bursting heart, he tightened his grip on the knife, and raised it, flashing in the sun.

Where is the lamb? In that desperate moment of the final decision he prepared to plunge the knife deep into the heart of the boy. But then—his hand was stopped. Behold, a lamb—a ram provided by God to take the place of Isaac.

I'm grateful that God provided a lamb for us—the Holy Lamb of God.

"Behold the lamb!" John says. Now I can crawl off the altar. Isaac may have forgotten his sixth birthday, or his first hunting trip, or his first romance, but I guarantee you one thing: he never forgot the day that God provided a substitute for his sacrifice.

The Bible says all who sin must die (see Romans 3:23; 6:23). I deserved to die on the altar, but God provided a lamb. "Look, the Lamb of God, who takes away the sin of the world!" (v. 29). Peter said, "He himself bore our sins in his body on the tree, so that we might die to sins and live for righteousness; by his wounds you have been healed. For you were like sheep going astray . . ." (1 Peter 2:25).

"For Christ died for sins once for all," (1 Peter 3:18). "I am the good shepherd. The good shepherd lays down his life for the sheep." (John 10:11) "He himself bore our sins . . ." (1 Peter 2:24).

If there is no lamb, then we must become the sacrifice. If there is no lamb, then we must bear the plunge of the knife. *But* —"Look, the Lamb of God, who takes away the sin of the world!" (v. 29). Isaiah said in Chapter 53 of his prophecy, "he took up our infirmities and carried our sorrows . . . he was crushed for our iniquities . . . by his wounds we are healed. The Lord has laid on him the iniquity of us all. He was led like a lamb to the slaughter, For he bore the sin of many, . . ." (vv. 4-12). Look, the lamb!

I like the way Twila Paris puts it in one of her songs on the album "Kingdom Seekers."

> Your only son no sin to hide
> Now you have sent him from your side.
> To walk upon this guilty sod
> And to become a Lamb of God
> Your gift of love they crucified
> They laughed and scorned him as he died
> The humble king they named a fraud
> And sacrificed the Lamb of God.
> I was so lost I should have died
> But you have brought me to your side
> To be on high your staff and rod
> And to become a lamb of God
>
> O Lamb of God, sweet Lamb of God

7

I love the holy Lamb of God
O wash me in his precious blood
My Jesus Christ, the Lamb of God.[1]

Incredible! Even as Christ became a Lamb, the Christian becomes a lamb. As we behold . . . we become! And so Jesus said to Peter, "Feed my lambs" (John 21:15).

WATCH THE LAMB

It is interesting that New Testament scholars place the timing of this passage just before the Passover. If you follow the sequence of the text it appears that John's announcement preceded the Passover by only a week or so: "the next day" (v. 35); "the next day" (v. 43); "the third day" (John 2:1); then the period immediately before Passover (v. 12).

That being the case, all the roads into Jerusalem would have been filled with pilgrims making their way to the city. And most every little group would have been bringing a little lamb . . . a lamb to sacrifice. The custom was to sacrifice one lamb for approximately every ten people. With the city's population swelling to some two million or more during this time, you can imagine how many lambs would be in the city.

From the time John the Baptist made his announcement, "Look, the lamb," three Passovers would be observed before the Lamb of God was sacrificed. Ray Boltz put it very dramatically in his song "Watch the Lamb" as he depicts Simon of Cyrene entering Jerusalem with his two small sons on that last Passover, carrying their lamb.

Walking on the road to Jerusalem
The time had come to sacrifice again.
My two small sons they walked beside me on the road.
The reason they came was to watch the lamb.
"Daddy, Daddy, what will we see there?
There's so much we don't understand."
So I told them of Moses and father Abraham.
And I said, "Dear children, WATCH THE LAMB."

For there will be so many in Jerusalem today.
We must be sure the lamb doesn't run away
And I told them of Moses and father Abraham.
And I said, "Dear children, WATCH THE LAMB."

We reached the city and I knew something must be wrong.
There were no joyful worshipers, no joyful worship songs.
I stood there with my children
In the midst of angry men.
And then I heard the crowd cry out,
"CRUCIFY HIM!"
We tried to leave the city, but we could not get away.
Forced to play in this drama
A part I did not want to play.
Why upon this day were men condemned to die?
Why were we standing here where soon they would pass by?

I looked up and said, "Even now they come."
The first one cried for mercy, the people gave him none.
The second one was violent, he was arrogant and loud.
I still can hear his angry voice screaming at the crowd.

Then someone said "there's Jesus" and I could scarce believe my eyes.

A man so badly beaten, he barely looked alive.
Blood poured from his body, from the thorns upon his brow . . .
Running down the cross and falling on the ground.

I watched Him as He struggled . . .
Watched Him as He fell.
The cross came down upon His back
The crowd began to yell.

In a moment I felt such agony
In a moment I felt such loss.
Until a Roman soldier grabbed my arm and said,
"YOU—CARRY HIS CROSS!"

At first I tried to resist him.
Then his hand reached for his sword.
And so I knelt and took the cross—from the Lord.
I placed it on my shoulder and started down the street.
The blood that He'd been shedding was running down my cheek.

They led Him to Golgotha.
They drove nails deep in His feet and hands.
And yet upon the cross I heard Him pray,
"FATHER, FORGIVE THEM!"

Oh, never have I seen such love in any other eyes.
"Into thy hands I commit my spirit"
And then He died.
I stood for what seemed like years; I'd lost all sense of time.
Until I felt two tiny hands holding tight to mine.
My children stood there weeping.
I heard the oldest say,

10

"Father, please forgive us
OUR LAMB JUST GOT AWAY!"

"Daddy, Daddy, what have we seen here?
There's so much we don't understand.
So I took them in my arms and we turned and faced the cross
And I said, "Dear children—WATCH THE LAMB!"[2]

THINK TIME

1. What does the symbol of the Lamb represent in your life?
2. What are some ways to focus on the Lamb?
3. How could you make the Lamb more important in your life?
4. Why was John the Baptist used to prepare the way for the Lamb?
5. Think of ways we become living sacrificial lambs.

[1]Twila Paris, "Lamb of God" from Album "Kingdom Seekers" (Houston: Star Song Records, 1985).
[2]Ray Boltz, "Watch The Lamb" from Album "Watch The Lamb" (Muncie, Indiana: Ray Boltz Ministries) n.d.

REVELATION 5:1-7

Then I saw in the right hand of him who sat on the throne a scroll with writing on both sides and sealed with seven seals. And I saw a mighty angel proclaiming in a loud voice, "Who is worthy to break the seals and open the scroll?" But no one in heaven or on earth or under the earth could open the scroll or even look inside . . . Then one of the elders said to me, "Do not weep! See, the Lion of the tribe of Judah, the Root of David, has triumphed. He is able to open the scroll and its seven seals."

Then I saw a Lamb, looking as if it had been slain, standing in the center of the throne, encircled by the four living creatures and the elders. He had seven horns and seven eyes, which are the seven spirits of God sent out into all the earth. He came and took the scroll from the right hand of him who sat on the throne.

2

When The Answers Don't Come

Revelation 5:1-7

"Then one of the elders said to me, 'Do not weep!
See, the Lion . . .' " (v. 5).

On a barren island ten miles long and five miles wide, forty miles off the coast of Asia Minor, an old man was caught up in the Spirit on Sunday and shown the revelation of Jesus Christ. The island was Patmos; the man was John (probably the apostle).

Never before had he witnessed such visual and auditory stimulation. He had seen the dead raised, lepers cleansed, and his Lord walk on the water, but never had he experienced anything like this.

The vision begins in Revelation 4. A great door in the sky is opened in the sky and John is brought through it and ushered into the throne room of God. There is lightning and rumbling peals of thunder. And then he saw God:

Holy, Holy, Holy
is the Lord God Almighty,
Who was, and is, and is to come! (Revelation 4:9).

15

And in his right hand there was a book—a scroll. It is locked shut with seven mighty seals.

The atmosphere is filled with tension as John becomes obsessed with vision of the scroll. The lightning and thunder set the stage with a most fearful backdrop, and like a television drama in which the background music grows louder and more intense, the suspense builds to a crescendo. A mighty angel suddenly appears and in a tone of utmost urgency shouts out a question in decibels that pierce every nook and cranny of the universe.

Who is worthy to open the book? It echoes through heaven, reaches every planet in the cosmos and surrounds the earth.

Who is worthy to open the book? The only response to the question is universal silence. No answer comes.

You may ask, "What book is this that draws the attention of heaven and earth?" This book represents the mind of God, and in it lies the answers to every question, every injury, every heartache, every problem. But as Revelation 5:3 points out, no answers are revealed. So many questions, all of which have answers, but no one is mighty enough to open the book and reveal the answers.

"Why did my baby die?" "Why did my husband leave me?" "Where did I go wrong?" "Will my boy ever return?" "Is there any hope?" So many questions; these and many, many more. But as verse 3 says, we will never know the answers. Life will forever remain a mystery, an enigma, an impossible puzzle.

Crisis reigns in heaven and on earth; as John gets caught up in this spirit of catastrophe, he begins to cry.

He says, "I wept and wept because no one was found who was worthy to open the scroll . . ." (v. 4). All of these questions are forever echoing in time, pleading for an answer, reverberating through the universe, never to be answered.

As I look back over my years in the ministry, I can remember so much of the heartache: the deaths, the

---

IN EVERY CASE WHEN WE BECOME CRISIS-CENTERED RATHER THAN CHRIST-CEN-TERED, WE ARE IN DANGER OF BEING LOST IN THE STORM.

---

funerals, the divorces, the runaways, the suicides, the sickness, the abuse, the tears, the pain—the questions. Each problem comes with its own set of questions. And, like John who weeps because the answers don't come, I have seen the tears of those who ask and seek. "Why won't somebody tell us why?" "Why won't somebody tell us where?" "Why won't somebody tell us how?"

I believe this passage in Revelation teaches us how to cope when the answers don't come. We are no strangers to trouble. We are susceptible to every ailment and burden to which the world is susceptible. The difference is, we know how to cope. We are taught the art of coping right here in Revelation 5.

The message is as relevant to us in this century as it was to those ancient Christians who were being slaughtered and persecuted for their faith. An answer is here when you lose your job, when you lose your loved one, when your marriage falls apart. The message here helps us to know what to do with the questions we have.

WATCH THE LION: WATCH THE LAMB

Many times our problems are unduly blown out of proportion because we haven't kept our eyes on the Lord. John is filled with agony of spirit when an elder comes to him and points him back to Jesus. If John the apostle is writing this (and I feel quite certain that he is), he perhaps remembers that stormy night in the small fishing boat on the Sea of Galilee, when Peter, impetuous as he was, asked Jesus to empower him to walk out on the undulating sea.

And Jesus told Peter to come; over the side of the boat Peter went to walk on the water to Jesus. As long as Peter kept his eyes on Jesus, he was able to maintain his stability in the midst of the storm. But when Galilee spit its cold spray up into his face and Peter took his eyes off the Lord, Peter began to be overcome by the storm and to sink in the waves. Taking his eyes off the Lord was almost a fatal mistake.

In every case when we become crisis-centered rather than Christ-centered, we are in danger of being lost in the storm. People involved in full-time supported ministry find this out rather quickly. An occupational hazard of the ministry is to become so involved with people that we take our eyes off the Lord. Whenever we do that, we are headed for a fall. The elder told John to get his eyes back on Jesus. The center of this vision is Jesus.

I believe in counseling, but it must be a style that is Christ-centered. Humanistic approaches to counseling, which rely on a multitude of manipulations to control and eventually heal the client, will usually end up with more questions and no answers. As a people we should be helping one another keep our eyes on Jesus. If we don't point people to Jesus, our time is wasted and ultimately no healing occurs.

Notice what John sees though when he finally turns to Jesus: first a lion; then a lamb. In verse 5 (of Revelation 5) he sees the Lion of Judah and then in verse 6 he sees a Lamb. The dualism here is wonderfully descriptive. He is *royalty*, yet he is *submissive*. He is *powerful*, yet he is *gentle*. He is *courageous*, yet he is *compassionate*. He is a *king*, yet he is a *sacrifice*. He has *majesty*, yet he has *meekness*.

For the Jewish reader, the message here is particularly rich. Whether this imagery of a Lion and a Lamb reminded him of the "lion's cub" of Genesis 49:9, or the Apocryphal Lion of 2 Esdras 12:31, or the lamb without blemish of 1 Peter 1:19, the Jew would be able to see in this image strength and compassion.

In times of crisis, you need help from someone who is both strong and gentle. That lesson was perhaps taught best in the Old Testament by Job. In that book (perhaps the oldest in the Bible) Job is portrayed as one in the storm of suffering and sickness. But he keeps his eyes on his Redeemer. He sees his Redeemer as one whose "wisdom is profound, his power is vast" (9:4), and "mighty, and firm in his purpose" (36:5).

THE LITTLE LAMB WITH SEVEN HORNS

What in the world could this mean? We must remember here that the Revelation is written in code language. The two attributes represented by the Lion and the Lamb are now coded into divine perfection and completion.

In the Bible the "horn" is a symbol of power and might. Seven is the code number in the Revelation for perfection. Seven horns means "perfect power." That

---

I BELIEVE I KNOW SOME CHRISTIANS WHO, IF GOD MOVED IN THEIR LIVES, THEY'D GO IMMEDIATELY INTO CARDIAC ARREST.

---

is, Jesus is all-powerful (omnipotent). Deuteronomy 33:17 describes the blessing of Moses as referring to the horns of Joseph giving Moses the power to push his people together to the ends of the earth. 1 Kings 22:11 tells us the story of the prophet Zedekiah making iron horns as a symbol of victory over the Syrians. Similar analogies can be found in Zechariah 1:1 and Psalm 75:4. In the time between the Testaments, the great heroes, of Israel were the Maccabees, the liberators. They were represented as horned lambs (1 Enoch 90:9).

The point here is that Christ is powerful enough to sustain us in the most chaotic storms of life. The most important question to be answered is whether or not we are going to trust Him completely with the answers to all our other questions. Do we really believe He has the power to sustain us in the times of our deepest need? Peter Marshall said, "Let our ulcers be our badges of unbelief."

I think most of us don't really put enough trust in the power of God. I'm reminded of the story I once heard about a little boy who was trying to go to sleep in his upstairs bedroom while a storm was raging outside. As the wind and the thunder and the lightning grew louder and more intense, he became increasingly afraid. Finally in desperation he ran downstairs and said, "Mommy, Mommy, I'm scared."

Her reply was only partially reassuring. "Don't be afraid, son; God is up there with you."

The boy, still trembling, made his way back up the stairs, cautiously crept over to the bed, and then slid all the way under the covers. In a few moments he peeped one eye out from under the cover and said, "God, if you are in here, please don't move 'cause you'd scare me to death."

I believe I know some Christians who, if God moved in their lives, they'd go immediately into cardiac arrest. But John is here reminding his readers of the complete power of Jesus. "Stop weeping!" the elder says. Have you forgotten how powerful the Lord is?

THE LITTLE LAMB WITH SEVEN EYES

Not only does this little lamb (the diminutive form is used in the Greek) have seven horns, representing perfect power, but he also has seven eyes, representing perfect knowledge. Perfect power is omnipotence and perfect knowledge is omniscience. He

21

can see everywhere because he is omnipresent. Because he can see everywhere he can be all-knowing. "Rise on the wings of the dawn" (Psalm 139:9), the psalmist said, "and go to the most distant place; God is there." We desperately need to practice the presence of God. My, how this would change our lives! Someone has written:

> Within thy circling power I stand
> And everywhere I find thy hand.
> Awake, asleep, at home abroad,
> I am surrounded still by God.

It is no wonder that when John was crying, the elder told him to look at Jesus. Jesus is the one who has the answers. He is the one who has the power to sustain us; the ability to understand us. Isaiah tells us that He is strong in power and understanding (Isaiah 40:26-28). Daniel said, "Wisdom and power are his" (Daniel 2:20). No wonder he is called "Wonderful Counselor."

Genesis 16:13 has been of particular help to me in times of great stress. Hagar said to the Lord, "You are the God who sees me, . . . I have now seen the One who sees me." The Greeks used to say that God is "All Eye." Our life is spent beneath the eye of God.

We need to understand the implication of this. The realization that God always sees us provides us not only with the motivation and incentive to do our best, but also the encouragement we need to face hard times. Realizing that God always sees us gives us security to face the storm and assurance when the answers don't come.

The Lamb of God: In His hand are all the answers. He is the one with perfect power (seven horns) and perfect knowledge (seven eyes).

He is omniscient—so nothing is invisible.
He is omnipotent—so nothing is impossible.

WATCH THE LAMB!

THINK TIME

1. What role does an all-seeing, all-knowing Lord play in your life?
2. What special power does Jesus have that should give us comfort in realizing he has the answers?
3. In what ways does Jesus give us counsel?
4. What can we do to help encourage our brothers and sisters to keep their eyes on the Lord?
5. If you were looking for a counselor to whom to refer a friend who is having problems, what special qualities would you want that counselor to possess?

JOHN 2:1-11

On the third day a wedding took place at Cana in Galilee. Jesus' mother was there, and Jesus and his disciples had also been invited to the wedding. When the wine was gone, Jesus' mother said to him, "They have no more wine." "Dear woman, why do you involve me?" Jesus replied, "My time has not yet come."

His mother said to the servants, "Do whatever he tells you."

Nearby stood six stone water jars, the kind used by the Jews for ceremonial washing, each holding from twenty to thirty gallons.

Jesus said to the servants, "Fill the jars with water"; so they filled them to the brim.

Then He told them, "Now draw some out and take it to the master of the banquet."

They did so, and the master of the banquet tasted the water that had been turned into wine. He did not realize where it had come from, though the servants who had drawn the water knew. Then he called the bridegroom aside and said, "Everyone brings out the choice wine first and then the cheaper wine after the guests have had too much to drink; but you have saved the best till now."

This, the first of His miraculous signs, Jesus performed in Cana of Galilee. He thus revealed his glory, and his disciples put their faith in him.

3

How To Enjoy The Party

John 2:1-11

"When the wine was gone, Jesus' mother said to him,
'They have no more wine' " (v. 3).

I don't want to just live; I want to *really* live.
I don't want to occasionally enjoy life; I want to have
constant joy in life. I don't know any adequate way to
do this outside Jesus. Jesus said, "I have come that they
may have life, and have it to the full" (John 10:10).

Jesus wants every Christian to get the most out of life.
Our view of Jesus as some kind of cosmic killjoy is
certainly unwarranted. The opposite is actually the case.
Jesus was one of the guests at this wedding party and
he wanted everyone to enjoy it to the fullest.

Becoming a Christian doesn't mean the end of joy.
The real truth is that when one becomes a Christian he
or she can begin to experience *real joy* in life. Yet we
often get the feeling that many Christians are not
experiencing the real joy of Jesus. Why is this? I heard
one man say of the appearance of some Christians, "I've
seen happier-looking faces on bottles of poison."

Christians (and congregations) who moan and groan
and fight and complain provide a better witness for the

devil than they do for the Lord. You go into some churches and you hear people criticize and argue and then watch them sit down and sing "O How I Love Jesus." A more appropriate song would probably be "The Fight Is On." Somehow their lives and their lips are so mismatched that a positive impression is not made upon unbelievers. We need to remember that one of the purposes of our assemblies is to impress the unbeliever (see 1 Corinthians 14:24-25).

As we get into this scripture we must remember that John called Jesus' action at Cana a sign (v. 11). John prefers to use the word *sign* in his Gospel instead of the word *miracle*. A sign is something that carries a message. It points out something of significance. We have often lost the real message of the miracle because we downgrade it to an argument for or against social drinking. That miracle cannot be used as a proof text for or against drinking liquor.

This sign has at least four messages in it. As we look at these messages in this chapter, it is important for us to realize that the "wedding party" in John 2 represents life. So when we consider "how to enjoy the party," we're really thinking about how to enjoy life.

MESSAGE #1: DON'T LIVE A LIE

In the Bible, wine is a symbol of joy (see Psalm 104:15). When Jesus turned the water into wine he was saying, in effect, "Your life should not just be routine; it should be wonderful." It's important to notice that the water Jesus turned into wine was not just drinking water, but it could be used for washing dirty hands and feet. In a sense, it was what we would call bath water.

Many people today are consuming vast amounts of bath water and then trying to convince themselves and others that they are really enjoying it. One look at the American culture ought to be enough to prove that true joy in this country is indeed a rare commodity. We are a culture gone crazy. Alcoholism is at epidemic proportions. Drug abuse is a national curse. Sexual promiscuity, even among teenagers, is rampant. AIDS has become a major phobia. One Menninger Foundation physician has stated that 30 million American children are in desperate need of immediate psychiatric attention. Some 70,000 teachers are assaulted every year. Around 4,000 babies a day are aborted. And perhaps the greatest national disease is loneliness. (By the way, people are not lonely because they are alone. They are lonely because they are empty inside.)

A legion of psychiatrists, psychologists, and psychotherapists don't seem to have helped us very much. It seems the more uninhibited we become the more we need the efforts of modern psychology. Some find their therapy at the local bar in "happy hour." But all the psychologists and all the happy hours in the world can't provide the joy that only Jesus can give.

But religion also has its bath water substitutes. John tells us that these six water jars were the ceremonial washbasins of the Jewish religion. Numbers are important in any of John's writings. The number seven, for example, is apocryphal code for perfection or completion. This is most clearly seen throughout the book of Revelation, but it also holds an important place in this Gospel. In the Gospel of John are seven signs Christ gives to prove that He is the Son of God. The number six also has a coded designation; it stands for "imperfection" or "incompletion."

Notice that there are six water pots. One message of this sign is that the old legalistic way is not the way to real happiness. What a shame it is that so many Christians try to be religious without Christ. We are not saved by the plan of salvation without the Man of salvation. You can know the plan of salvation and still not be saved. Legalism is nothing more than bath water and it simply won't suffice at Jesus' party.

MESSAGE #2: DON'T SETTLE FOR BATH WATER

Not only does Jesus give *real* joy but He gives plenty of it. Christians should not settle for less than what Jesus wants us to have. Jesus can give us the change we need in our life and He can give it to us with abundant power.

What a sign for Jesus to use to inaugurate His ministry! Moses began his ministry by turning water into blood as a sign of death. Jesus begins His ministry by turning water into wine, a sign of life and joy. If you are an habitual complainer and pessimist, if you're always looking on the dark side, if you can never find anything good about life, then maybe Jesus hasn't begun His ministry in you yet.

Notice first that the change is an instantaneous one. In verse 7 it's water; in verse 10, wine. We take instantaneous change for granted. I can pick up the telephone and speak with someone on the other side of the world as quickly as someone across the street. I flew out of Dulles International Airport recently on a flight that departed at 3 p.m. and arrived in St. Louis at 2:55 p.m. Instantaneous activity is something we too often take for granted, forgetting that it has not always been like that.

The real wonder in this miracle is not that water becomes wine. Water can become wine quite naturally. Water comes down from heaven in the form of rain, flows through the ground where it is absorbed by roots of the vine and then is drawn up through the stem where it chemically reacts with various agents, swells out the fruit into clusters and then is squeezed into wine. This takes months—years, when you count the growing of the vine. But Jesus changed the water into wine instantly. Jesus can also change your life instantly. He can change it from water to wine; from a child of Satan to a child of God.

An important element of this miracle should not be overlooked. Jesus had the cooperation of the people at the wedding. First, they wanted the wine; and second, they were willing to do what the Lord told them to do. "How to Enjoy the Party" is translated for us into "How to Enjoy Life." The pattern in this miracle is first, do you want real joy? And second, are you willing to do whatever Jesus asks you to do? Both questions are critical. Are you willing to cooperate with Jesus in the making of the miracle?

But doesn't everybody want happiness? A psychological principle called secondary gain suggests that the way some people get attention is by constantly expressing their unhappiness. If you take away their unhappiness, in their way of thinking, you take away the attention they receive from other people. Have you ever known someone whose every conversation is consumed with all their sicknesses? Subconsciously they realize that if they didn't have all those health problems, they would have nothing to talk about. So the first prerequisite in the miracle is that people have to want the joy that Jesus has to offer.

The second prerequisite is that they have to be willing to do what Jesus asks them to do. Suppose one of the servants in this miracle had said, "Surely, Lord, you don't want one of the water jars. I'll bring you one of our flower vases."

WITH JESUS THE BEST IS ALWAYS YET TO COME. FIRST THE WATER; THEN THE WINE. FIRST THE OLD LAW, WHICH LED TO DEATH; THEN THE NEW COVENANT, WHICH LEADS TO LIFE. FIRST MOSES, WHO TURNED WATER TO BLOOD; THEN JESUS, WHO TURNED WATER TO WINE.

You may say, "That's ridiculous." But we do it all the time in the area of religion. Whether it's changing His commandments on baptism, or church attendance, or something else, many Christians seem to think that they have a better way. A few years ago one large church convention decreed that hamburgers and Coke would be permissible for communion services for youth groups since it displayed greater cultural relevance.

Verse 5 says, "Do whatever he tells you." Before the water can change to wine, we have to be willing to do whatever He tells us.

When Jesus makes the change, notice the generosity of the miracle. In verse 6 we discover that He made about 150 gallons of wine for this party. He certainly wasn't stingy with His power. The reader of John's Gospel should not be surprised at the abundance of Jesus' supply. Jesus said in John 1:3 that all things were made by Him. With a few loaves and fish He fed an entire multitude in Chapter 6. No wonder He could make such a large quantity of wine!

But isn't this just like Jesus, doing everything on such a large and generous scale? I like the way Dewitt Talmage put it. "When Christ the Creator went forth to make leaves, he made them by the forest full. When he went forth to make flowers, he made plenty of them, flaming from hedges, hanging from clinging vines, sprawling down garden paths, rolling in waves of lavish color. When he went forth to create water, it was not by the cupful but by the rivers full and the lakes full, and the ocean full. And when he provides salvation it's not a little salvation for this one and that one. But it's in sufficient abundance for all."[1] And when He pours out His joy, there's more than enough to go around.

A little boy from a very large, very poor family was injured in a traffic accident. He was taken to the local hospital, where a nurse brought him a large glass of milk. His question was "How deep shall I drink?" He'd been accustomed to having to share with his brother and sister.

The nurse, sensing this, said "You drink as deep as you want, and if you want more, there's plenty where that came from."

That's what Jesus is saying in this miracle. "There's plenty more where that came from."

MESSAGE #3: SAVE THE BEST FOR LAST

Notice verse 10: "Everyone brings out the choice wine first and then the cheaper wine." That's the way it usually is with life, isn't it? Friendship often begins with "honey-love" talk and ends with lines of hatred drawn like swords and shields. In the Old Testament, Ahithophel first served David with loving devotion, and then he became a traitor (see 1 Samuel 15-17; 1 Chronicles 27). Judas walked with Jesus, then betrayed Him with a kiss on the cheek (see Matthew 26:49; Mark 14:15).

Sin is like that. It says, "Sleep with me. Go to bed with me. I'll take you to paradise." But the artificial highs of the world's wines never last. The highs never quite equal the lows of the morning after. A life without Jesus is like that. It starts off with all the vitality and energy of youth, but without Jesus it grows old and hopeless. And there's nothing drearier in the whole world than a godless old age.

With Jesus the best is always yet to come. First the water; then the wine. First the Old Law, which led to death; then the New Covenant, which leads to life. First Moses, who turned water to blood; then Jesus, who turned water to wine. In the old dispensation the Israelites ate their manna in the wilderness. Today we partake of the Bread that came down from heaven. They drank from water that came from the rock. Ours is the living water, of which when men drink, they shall never thirst again. Theirs was the shadow; ours is the reality. For the Christian the best is always yet to come.

MESSAGE #4: DO IT JESUS' WAY

"They have no more wine," Mary said (v. 3). In every person's life there comes a time when the wine of happiness, enthusiasm, and exhilaration is gone. Every time I preach, I realize that I am probably speaking to a number of people in whose lives the wine has run out. Are you happier now than you used to be? Are you enjoying life more than ever before? Are you as excited about your relationships with people as you used to be? Are you as excited about your relationship with God as you once were? If not, maybe it's because for you the wine is gone.

In this miracle the answer for restoring the wine is found. If you're tired of the rat race and the routine and are wanting to rejoin the party, a four-step process is here for you. In these four steps one finds the way to open up the flow of God's love and mercy.

Step 1. Recognize your need. "They have no more wine" (v. 3). Jesus has always required a confession of need before He will work in one's life. Mary is saying, "We need you, Jesus." Don't expect the water to change to wine until confession of need is expressed.

Step 2. Obey His commands. "Do whatever he tells you" (v. 5). Before the blessing comes the command. Before the blind man receives his sight, he has to go wash in Siloam. Before the withered arm is healed, it must first reach out to Jesus. Before Naaman is cleansed, he must first obey the command to dip in the Jordan seven times. The water would not have been made into wine without the filling of the water pots. Jesus will not change our lives without unquestioned obedience.

Step 3. Serve Him zealously. "Jesus said to the servants, 'Fill the jars with water'; so they filled them to the brim" (v. 7). You see, there is a way to fill a container, and there is a way to *really* fill a container. A container is considered full before it reaches the brim. The message here is whatever you do, do it to the brim. When you serve Him, serve Him with all your heart.

Step 4. Depend completely upon Christ. Unquestioned obedience is not what changes the water to wine. K.C. Moser used to say, "There's not a might of merit in a million works of men." How true that is. Our action without God's work never results in water being changed to wine. It is Jesus who converts both water to wine and sinner to saved.

It's not hard to live the Christian life. It's impossible! Impossible, that is, without Jesus. Only Jesus can make the necessary changes in us.

And that's
   the only way
      I can enjoy the party!

THINK TIME

1. Discuss the symbolic nature of the "wedding party."
2. What is the symbolism of the "wine" in this passage?
3. What worldly "highs" have you been substituting for the real "high" offered by Jesus?
4. Where do you **normally turn** for help in a crisis?
5. Are you **constantly cooperating** with Jesus? If not, what can you do to change this? How can Jesus help?

---

[1]T. Dewitt Talmage, *500 Selected Sermons* (Grand Rapids: Baker Book House, 1957), pp. 337-347.

JOHN 3:1-16

Now there was a man of the Pharisees named Nicodemus, a member of the Jewish ruling council. He came to Jesus at night and said, "Rabbi, we know you are a teacher who has come from God. For no one could perform the miraculous signs you are doing if God were not with him."

In reply Jesus declared, "I tell you the truth, no one can see the kingdom of God unless he is born again."

"How can a man be born when he is old?" Nicodemus asked. "Surely he cannot enter a second time into his mother's womb to be born!"

Jesus answered, "I tell you the truth, no one can enter the kingdom of God unless he is born of water and the Spirit. Flesh gives birth to flesh, but the Spirit gives birth to spirit. You should not be surprised at my saying, 'You must be born again.' The wind blows wherever it pleases. You hear its sound, but you cannot tell where it comes from or where it is going. So it is with everyone born of the Spirit."

"How can this be?" Nicodemus asked.

"You are Israel's teacher," said Jesus, "and do you not understand these things? I tell you the truth, we speak of what we know, and we testify to what we have seen, but still you people do not accept our testimony. I have spoken to you of earthly things and you do not believe; how then will you believe if I speak of heavenly things? No one has ever gone into heaven except the one who came from heaven—the Son of Man. Just as Moses must be lifted up, that everyone who believes in him may have eternal life."

"For God so loved the world that he gave his one and only Son, that whoever believes in him shall not perish but have eternal life . . ."

4

God Is A Gambler

John 3:1-16

Conservative Christians have generally spoken out long and hard against the vices of gambling, and rightly so! The slot machines, casinos, and parimutuels have contributed greatly to the downfall of our nation's morals. The church's voice is greatly needed in this area and it needs to be to the tune of a resounding NO!

I read the other day that the English church in Monaco will not sing a hymn whose number is lower than 37 for fear that the hunch players in the congregation will rush out to back that number at the local casino. New Zealand churches faced a similar problem when it became a custom for some church members to place bets on the hymns to be selected for the following Sunday.

Gambling has always downgraded the values of any community or nation. Did you read about the county sheriff who confiscated all the slot machines in his county on the basis of a law that banned the use of steel traps for catching dumb animals? Really!

Christianity Today reported the case of an unlucky Salvation Army solicitor whose relative gave him a lottery ticket that won $30,000. He was immediately dismissed from the Salvation Army.

But this is not the kind of gambling I want us to consider in this chapter. The kind of gambling that we are now concerned with is for the highest stakes of all: eternity. With these thoughts in mind, let's notice three facts about Christian gambling.

GOD IS A GAMBLE

Blaise Pascal in his famous work *Penseés* (or *Thoughts*) says in effect that God is a wager. You not only bet your life, but you also bet your soul. Another philosopher put it this way: We all bet on God; that He exists or that He doesn't. If He does exist, then there is a winner and a loser. If He doesn't exist, then both are losers. Thus the only way to win is to bet on His existence. To bet against His existence is to be a loser in either case.

Helmut Thielicke, the famous German preacher, put it most succinctly when he wrote:

What does it mean to put your passions on the line when you bet on God? In simple terms it means that I carry out an experiment with God. I act temporarily and tentatively "as if God existed." To act "as if" God existed means I play the role of a believer. I behave toward my neighbor "as if" the word of God about loving your neighbor as yourself were really in effect. I deal with my cares "as if" someone were there on whom I could cast them. I forgive my fellow man "as if" God forgave me and I had to hand on the gift I had received. I pray "as if" God were there to hear me. But how will God react when I perform my experiment with Him and agree to bet? If He is the one His witnesses confess Him to be, He will let me know that it was no empty game or masquerade. My willingness to play for high stakes proved that I did not want to have my life to myself. God lets Himself be found (Jeremiah 29:13) by people who put their lives on the line. Having done that I have made the first move in the wager. Now it's God's turn. In the moment I will see if He is and who He is. That is the wager on God.[1]

John 3:14-21 is one of those places in the New Testament where the "windows are open" for Christian betting. "For God so loved the world" (John 3:16). We wager for or against His exorbitance; we wager for or against His love. In the same verse we wager for or against the reality of eternal life: "Whoever believes in him shall not perish but have eternal life."

In numerous other places in the New Testament one can see the wager with clarity. In the parable of the Good Samaritan a lawyer asks Jesus, "What must I do to inherit eternal life?" (Luke 10:25). The stakes are eternal life. The bet in this case was social involvement. If you're willing to get involved in the wretchedness of society, the dirty parts, the sickness, the wounds, the bigotry, the hatred, to do something about it . . . to risk your life . . . for eternal life . . . that's THE WAGER.

In Luke 18:18 THE WAGER is once again clearly presented. The same question asked by the lawyer in Luke 10 is this time posed by a rich young ruler: "What must I do to inherit eternal life?" In Jesus' response we get a picture of the gamble that a person who seeks eternal life must make. In this case Jesus says that we must be willing to put our possessions (or what Lloyd Ogilvie calls our "thingdoms") on the line. It is when one becomes willing to sacrifice the things of this life in order to risk care from an unseen source that one can bet on eternal life. This then is the wager!

I cannot find God with my physical senses. I cannot pragmatically prove His existence. But as Gerald Kennedy says, a person can't "live for ten minutes on the basis of what he can prove." God is a gamble. If He exists, believers win; unbelievers lose. If He doesn't, both lose. In any case, the unbeliever loses. But also . . .

GOD IS A GAMBLER

God is not only a gamble, He is also a gambler. Think about the ways He has gambled. He created man for fellowship, betting that some would choose to have a relationship with Him. He also risked the possibility of rejection! No one has to fellowship with God! He revealed Himself to us, risking Himself . . . betting that some of us would fall in love with Him. At the same time exposing Himself to ridicule, denial, and rebellion.

Each new person is a gamble for God. We understand how that works with our children. With every new child that we bring into this world we gamble that we can bring them to faith. Martin Luther and his wife Katie had a baby. In a letter to the prospective godmother, Luther wrote, "God has produced in me and my wife Katie a little heathen. We hope you will be willing to become her spiritual mother and help make her a Christian."[2]

Bishop Kennedy said in response to this statement by Luther, "God is like that. He takes us as we are, hesitating between the mud and the stars, and like a father, He gambles on His children by giving them freedom."[3] "For God so loved the world that he gave his one and only Son, that whoever believes in Him shall not perish but have eternal life" (John 3:16). If you decide to bet on God, the only kind of God you can believe in is a God who gambles.

THE GAMBLER ON THE CROSS

All the way through the Gospels, Jesus is a gambler. Even His unique entry into this planet poses stakes so high that we can't even begin to comprehend. Think of it—our God—a baby in the straw. Think about the gamble of going about finding disciples, not one of whom had to follow Him. Everyone of them could have rejected Him. Never did He destroy free moral will.

And then He went against the Prince of Darkness time and time again, going to the cross, believing in believers, risking everything in hopes that when He came back again He would find faith (Luke 18:8), gambling His life in order to give eternal life, betting His life that His death would be redemptive.

It is on the cross that we most clearly see the ultimate wager. Let's look at it again.

Finally Pilate handed him over to them to be crucified. So the soldiers took charge of Jesus. Carrying his own cross, he went out to the place of the Skull (which in Aramaic is called Golgotha). Here they crucified him . . . When the soldiers crucified Jesus, they took his clothes, dividing them into four shares, one for each of them, with the undergarment remaining. This garment was seamless, woven in one piece from top to bottom. "Let's not tear it," they said to one another. "Let's decide by lot who will get it." This happened that the scripture might be fulfilled which said, "They divided my garments among them and cast lots for my clothing" (John 19:16-18; 23-24).

Do you see it? They're all gamblers. But do you see the contrast? The cheap, heartless, tawdry gamblers at the foot of the cross with the strange man on the cross making the heroic gamble. He's "betting His life that love is stronger than hate, that life will conquer death,

---

EACH NEW PERSON IS A GAMBLE FOR GOD. WE UNDERSTAND HOW THAT WORKS WITH OUR CHILDREN. WITH EVERY NEW CHILD THAT WE BRING INTO THE WORLD WE GAMBLE THAT WE CAN BRING THEM TO FAITH.

---

that God seeks and forgives. It will be too bad if we lose sight of the risk He took at Calvary, for the stakes were never higher and the daring courage shown never greater. When you think about men running risks for higher stakes, think of Jesus."[4]

Amazing! God gambles on us and we have the power to make God a winner or a loser. He honors us with that power. We call it free moral agency. But an essential difference exists between this kind of gambling and the gambling in the casinos of this world. In God's case, and for each of us, if God wins, we win; if He loses, we lose.

The wager is up to us.

THINK TIME

1. In what ways has God gambled in your life?
2. In what ways have you gambled on God?
3. Discuss the irony of "The Gambler on the cross."
4. What does it mean to give birth to faith by living and acting "as if" God exists?
5. What are some risks you can take for Christ?

[1]Helmut Thielicke, *How To Believe Again* (Philadelphia: Fortress Press, 1970), pp. 18-19.
[2]Roland Bainton, *Here I Stand* (Abingdon-Cokesbury, 1950), p. 293.
[3]Gerald Kennedy, "Gamblers at the Cross," in *Best Sermons*, ed. G. Paul Butler (New York: The MacMillan Company, 1952), p. 123.
[4]Ibid., p. 121.

LUKE 7:1-10

When Jesus had finished saying all this in the hearing of the people, he entered Capernaum. There a centurion's servant, whom his master valued highly, was sick and about to die. The centurion heard of Jesus and sent some elders of the Jews to him, asking him to come and heal his servant. When they came to Jesus, they pleaded earnestly with him, "This man deserves to have you do this, because he loves our nation and has built our synagogue." So Jesus went with them.

He was not far from the house when the centurion sent friends to say to him: "Don't trouble yourself, for I do not deserve to have you come under my roof. That is why I did not even consider myself worthy to come to you. But say the word, and my servant will be healed. For I myself am a man under authority, with soldiers under me. I tell this one, 'Go,' and he goes; and that one, 'Come,' and he comes. I say to my servant, 'Do this,' and he does it."

When Jesus heard this, he was amazed at him, he said, "I tell you, I have not found such great faith even in Israel." Then the men who had been sent returned to the house and found the servant well.

5

Just Say The Word

Luke 7:1-10

"But say the word, and my servant will be healed"
(v. 7).

*H*ave you ever wondered what Jesus'
voice sounded like? I wonder if He was a bass or a tenor.
I wonder if He sounded dramatically authoritative, or
perhaps rather meek and gentle. I wonder if He
normally talked loudly or softly. Was His voice more of
a whisper or more of a roar? Was it somewhere in
between?

I wonder what His voiceprints would look like.
Voiceprints are as unique as fingerprints; they are a
sound analysis that reflects important qualities of a
speaker's voice as determined by his throat structure. I
wonder what element of Jesus' speaking voice enabled
Him to receive such rapt attention.

Luke 19:48 says people "hung on his words." Luke
4:22 says the people were "amazed at the gracious
words that came from his lips." John 6:63 says, "The
words I have spoken to you are spirit and they are life."
In John 6:68 Peter says, "You have the words of eternal
life."

Words are important! It took a full-scale civil war to change the number of one verb in this country. Before the U.S. Civil War, the term *United States* was always used with a plural verb: the United States *are*. Since the Civil War, the singular verb has always been employed: the United States *is*.

Medicine at Work, a journal published by the Pharmaceutical Manufacturers Association, warns doctors to be very careful with the way they use words. An anesthetist should not say, "I'm going to shoot him

---

WE ARE NOT ULTIMATELY IN BONDAGE TO THE NATURAL PROCESSES OF THIS WORLD. WE HAVE A SUPERNATURAL RELIGION. WE HAVE A TRANSCENDENT SAVIOR!

---

now." Can you imagine the reaction those words could receive?

The average person speaks about 25,000 words daily. The fastest speech recorded from a politician was from President John F. Kennedy in 1961 at 327 words per minute. The woman's nonstop talking record is held by Mary E. Davis, who talked straight for 110 hours and 30 minutes. I'd hate to sit next to her on an airplane—or, even worse, on a bus.

But what did Jesus' words sound like? In Luke 7:7 a Gentile centurion sends word to Jesus to "say the word." Let's think for just a moment about the context of this statement.

First of all, the incident took place in Capernaum. Jesus had made Capernaum the headquarters for His Galilean ministry. No small rural village, Capernaum was the home of a large Roman military unit and was situated on a major north-south passageway. It's quite possible that Jesus stayed in Peter's house and performed many miracles in Capernaum.

How unusual to find faith in a Roman centurion! He is a Gentile, a military man. Rome placed a great deal of confidence in her centurions. They had to be a special breed of men. Charles H. Spurgeon said, regarding this man, "We may find the choicest flowers blooming where we least expected them. The best pearls have been found in the darkest caves." It's interesting to note here that all the centurions mentioned in the New Testament are mentioned in a favorable light.

Verse 9 helps us realize that quite a crowd had gathered around the Lord. Jesus often attracted a crowd, and you can count on the fact that the people didn't come out of guilt or obligation, or to make up for a time they missed. They came because they were excited to be in His presence.

The floor of the synagogue mentioned in verse 5 was excavated in 1905. You can see almost the exact spot where Jesus stood and taught.

All this provides us with the backdrop for a most unusual event which culminates in the wonderful commendation of the centurion by Jesus: "I tell you, I have not found such great faith even in Israel" (v. 9). Jesus commended the centurion because this man did not require the physical presence of Jesus to have faith in His power. He simply needed the *word*. Now let's notice something about that *word.*

THE WORD OF POWER

The words of Christ have always been founded on the great power of Christ. Remember the words of Christ brought this universe into existence (see John 1:3; Colossians 1:15-16). His lips moved and the planets spun into orbit; the sun burst into flame; the solar system took on order. His lips moved again and our planet began to be inhabited by living things. His words turned cemeteries into places of celebration, harlots into heralds of the gospel, and strong soldiers into weaklings. What words! What wonderful words! What powerful words!

His words possessed specific power over specific laws of nature. Jesus never was in subjugation to nature. He

---

THINK OF WHAT WOULD HAPPEN IF WE ALL REALLY GOT SERIOUS ABOUT THE WORDS OF JESUS!

---

created nature. Living in a culture today that is largely rooted in naturalism, we find it hard to understand the full impact of Jesus' power over nature. We are not ultimately in bondage to the natural processes of this world. We have a supernatural religion. We have a transcendent Savior. The word of Christ has ultimate and supreme power over nature.

He could speak the word and a dying slave would be healed. He could speak the word and the weather would change. He could speak the word and dead bodies would regain life and open their eyes. He could speak the word and sick people would be cured.

And He can still do it! We've become so rabid against the "faith healers" we may have forgotten that Jesus can still heal. His power has not declined. If He can't or if He doesn't, let's quit making a mockery out of our prayers by asking Him to do it. Now that's not to say He always does it. He didn't then and He doesn't now. His purposes are beyond us, but let's not limit His power! Just because He has His own agenda doesn't mean He can't or doesn't ever heal today.

If you believe in Christ, believe in a powerful Christ—a Christ who can still do something. He still has the power over all nature. "Say the word, and my servant will be healed" (v. 7).

Jesus also has the power over cultural barriers. Jesus was sent to the Jews (see Matthew 15:24), and this centurion was a Gentile. The gateway for salvation was not to be opened for the Gentiles until another centurion by the name of Cornelius came to the Lord years later. Jews hated Gentiles, but here we see Jesus breaking through a cultural barrier of His love for all people.

Notice also the splendid example of the centurion. Can you imagine this Roman military officer humbling himself to this itinerant Jew? The hardest lessons for Americans to learn are those of submission and humility. Jesus exercised His power when this man of authority and power humbled Himself. Have you really humbled yourself to Jesus? In our affluent and advanced culture our tendency is to be arrogant, not only to other ethnic groups but also to Christ. Jesus' words had power over nature and culture.

THE WORD OF RESTORATION

Jesus also spoke words of restoration and reconciliation. This centurion had at least two reasons for wanting his dearly loved servant healed. He wanted what was best for the man, but also he wanted his loving and normal relationship with the servant restored. Sickness had interrupted it. This centurion held his servant in honor. The word here means that he cherished his servant and held him dear to his heart. The same word is used in Luke 14:8, Philippians 2:29, and 1 Peter 2:4-6. This Gentile did not want the relationship to end. He earnestly begged through his friends and elders of the Jews for a word from Jesus so he could keep his friend.

What would it be like if we held our Christian relationships in such high esteem that we continually sought a word from Jesus to keep those relationships strong and healthy? What would it be like if we humbled ourselves and submitted ourselves and did anything possible to allow Jesus to be the Savior of our relationships?

References to sickness in the Bible are often symbolic of sin. How many times do we lose a brother or a sister to the sickness of sin? How many times do we let them go rather than make an all-out effort to restore the relationship? We need to be like the centurion and do whatever is necessary to bring about the power of Jesus to save that relationship.

Recently I met a preacher who related to me a most remarkable experience. While he was preaching one Sunday morning, one of his elders walked down the aisle in the middle of his sermon right up to his side.

The elder asked him, "Fred, do you trust me?" The preacher responded in the affirmative and yielded the pulpit to the elder.

This man of God then began to read Matthew 5:23-24. "Therefore, if you are offering your gift at the altar and there remember that your brother has something against you, leave your gift there in front of the altar. First go and be reconciled to your brother; then come and offer your gift."

This elder then said, "Ten years ago this church split from another congregation in this town. Since then there have been a lot of hard feelings between our two congregations. We need to make it right."

He then proceeded to talk about the importance of restoring the relationship. Finally he suggested they all get in their cars and go to the other congregation and make things right.

One member, noticing the long line of cars, commented, "Man, this looks like a funeral procession!"

One of his fellow travelers replied, "It is. We're all dying to ourselves."

They all went to the other congregation's building and when the preacher extended the invitation at the end of his sermon, this entire visiting congregation responded by going forward. I asked Fred if every member of his congregation went forward at the invitation. "Everyone except the Pharisees," he said. I guess every church has some Pharisees. But what a wonderful example of submission to the words of Jesus. These words from Jesus in Matthew 5 healed a sickness of sin and brought reconciliation to these two churches.

Think of what would happen if we all really got serious about the words of Jesus! Think of the dramatic

effect it could have on people's lives if entire congregations paid visits to members who were beginning to
leave the relationships, who were becoming sick in the
sins of this world. I preach for a congregation that has
well over a thousand members. What would happen if,
every time a teen-ager came in drunk, or a marriage
began to break-up, or a businessman yielded to
temptation, or a member became discouraged, or a
member started getting spiritually sick, we took the
words of Jesus so seriously that over one thousand of
us paid visits to that person that week? I wonder how
many souls might be saved; how many relationships
might be healed; how many marriages might be
rescued. The first step is to submit ourselves and go to
Jesus for a word of power and a word of restoration.

THE WORD OF HEALING

The servant was healed by the words of Jesus; there
was no need for His physical presence. His words alone
were enough to bring healing power to the people. The
English word *heal* is translated from a Greek word that
can be also translated by the word *save*.

What Jesus' words did physically for the centurion's
servant, they can do spiritually for each of us. His words
can bring redemptive power as well as physical power.
What we need is the humility to be completely
submissive to His words. Healing is one thing we need
in our twentieth-century culture. Wounds are deep in
families, churches, and persons; wounds are national
and international. The answer to these wounds is not
in the newest fad of psychology. It is not to be found

in this world's media or education. Healing can only be found in Jesus. Never before have we needed the words of Jesus more desperately than we do today.

The problem is not a problem of the impotence of His words. The problem is our lack of commitment to humble ourselves before His Word. The writing of this book was originally composed on a word processing computer, a machine that deals literally and technically with words. Perhaps this is the approach we need to take coming to Jesus. We need to process His words in our hearts quite literally and quite technically. It is only then that healing can occur in our lives.

Look at verse 9: "When Jesus heard this (that is, the words of the centurion), he was amazed at him, and turning to the crowd following Him, he said, 'I tell you, I have not found such great faith even in Israel.' " Notice particularly the phrase, "he was amazed at him." What a compliment! Often in the Gospels we find occasions where people were amazed at Jesus. Here is an occasion where Jesus is amazed at someone.

Wouldn't you like to hear Jesus say someday "_____, back there on earth, during your lifetime, I was amazed at you." What was it that caused the centurion to be so amazing? It was his utter faith . . .

in the power . . .

of the words of Jesus.

Do you have utter faith?

THINK TIME

1. In what ways has God provided healing to you in the past? Be specific.
2. What words of the Lord Jesus have had the greatest impact on your life?
3. What lesson can the centurion teach us?
4. Discuss the healing process that the words of God can provide for us emotionally, spiritually, and physically.

MATTHEW 15:21-28

Leaving that place, Jesus withdrew to the region of Tyre and Sidon. A Canaanite woman from that vicinity came to him, crying out, "Lord, Son of David, Have mercy on me! My daughter is suffering terribly from demon-possession."

Jesus did not answer a word. So his disciples came to him and urged him, "Send her away, for she keeps crying out after us."

He answered, "I was sent only to the lost sheep of Israel."

The woman came and knelt before him. "Lord, help me!" she said.

He replied, "It is not right to take the children's bread and toss it to their dogs."

"Yes, Lord," she said, "but even the dogs eat the crumbs that fall from their masters' table."

Then Jesus answered, "Woman, you have great faith! Your request is granted." And her daughter was healed from that very hour.

6

When God Is Silent

Matthew 15:21-28

*R*eading through this story is like walking down a dark alley. Shadows could hide frightening things and we are afraid that at any moment we might be overpowered by something we don't understand. Basically, we are afraid of silence.

Our junior high and high school age young men were recently in charge of our Wednesday evening service, and presented many good speeches, songs, prayers, and readings. But when Paul Watts got up to speak, he stunned everyone. His opening words were, "I owe this congregation and youth group an apology. I'm just not prepared to speak tonight."

He promptly sat down. For about two minutes nothing happened. No one got up to take his place. No elder came up to encourage and restart the service. For about two long minutes there was nothing but silence, deafening silence! Finally Paul returned to the pulpit and delivered a splendid lesson on "Being Prepared." The audience was extremely relieved.

Silence is difficult to bear. It is especially difficult for us to contemplate the silence of God and wonder what it means. We are accustomed to His miracles; they really

don't frighten us the way they should. We have **effectively denuded them** of any present relevance.

We like to talk about His power, though we generally **tend to do so sparingly.** His power doesn't frighten us. His death doesn't scare us. It's history. His resurrection isn't frightening. Years of Easter sermons have neutralized in our minds the real drama of the empty tomb.

But His silence bothers us—because we don't know what it means. How many times has each of us confronted the silence of God? How many of us, like the parent in this story, have gone to Jesus in behalf of a child or a parent or a spouse or a loved one who is under the control of Satan, only to be met with the silence of God?

Seldom in the Bible do we encounter the silence of God. Jesus' birth provided the only occasion I know for a special presentation of the heavenly chorus of angels. His baptism and transfiguration were affirmed by the voice of God. Often the Gospels introduce a teaching of Jesus with "He opened his mouth and taught them, saying . . ."

But there are also some dreadful moments of silence. The God who split the air at the Mount of Transfiguration with, "This is my Son, whom I love" (Matthew 17:5) was silent at Calvary, evoking from Jesus some of His most difficult to understand words: "My God, my God, why have you forsaken me?" (Matthew 27:46). The whole universe was so uncomfortable with the silence of heaven that the earth shook violently and the sun hid its face.

This story is the only record we have of Jesus' leaving the borders of Israel. One writer calls this story "one of the most profound and unfathomable stories of the New

Testament." It is that way because of Jesus' response (or perhaps I should say, lack of response). In the original the negative is emphatic. It's not an accidental silence.

It's even more confusing, given the desperate condition of this poor mother who has come in behalf of her demonized daughter. Chrysostom describes her behavior as an act of "beautiful shamelessness." There she is, on her knees, worshipping God. The Greek word in verse 25 that is translated "knelt" is one of the words

---

IT IS ESPECIALLY DIFFICULT FOR US TO CONTEMPLATE THE SILENCE OF GOD AND WONDER WHAT IT MEANS.

---

used in the New Testament for "worship." This woman worshipped the Lord and He responded only in silence.

Why is Jesus silent? There are several possibilities. First let's notice what His silence does not mean.

SILENCE DOES NOT MEAN . . .

That no work is being accomplished. God can still work in silence. The very hour that the Father was most silent in response to the crying Christ on Calvary was the very hour that He secured our redemption. Silence does not mean a lack of love or care or activity.

While God's words are important, His words are nothing without His works. The Beatitudes, the Sermon on the Mount, the parables all would be meaningless without God's redemptive work. When we take our struggles to God, and are confronted by His silence, it does not mean that He is not working.

Helmut Thielicke, a powerful and popular preacher in Germany during World War II, preached for the large cathedral church in Stuttgart. He was away in Dodensee when the Allied forces bombed Stuttgart. He returned immediately, took the train as far into the city as he could go, got off the train and asked a station attendant, "Where is Stuttgart?"

The attendant pointed to the great pillar of smoke and said, "There is Stuttgart!"

Describing that moment later, Thielicke wrote, "We had to walk from Connstatt making our way through a stream of refugees—old people, women and children who were all going the other way, their faces marked by horror, dirty and in the strangest assortment of clothing. Perhaps worse than the disasters themselves is the reflection in the eyes of men. The reflection prepared us inwardly to such an extent that when we saw our burning house and even the glowing ruins of Stiftskirche, we were not so much affected as we would otherwise have been."[1]

His collection of sermons that came from this period of time was called *The Silence of God.* He preached "in broken pulpits under shattered spires to hearers who were scattered to the winds and to every kind of hopelessness." His message was that while God may be silent, he has not quit working.

His silence also does not mean . . . *a reluctance on His part to work in some people's lives, but not in others.* The Bible makes it clear that whosoever will may come (see

Mark 8:34). God is love, but love is sometimes silent. So then, what does this event in the Lord's life mean?

WHY WAS JESUS SILENT?

To show us who we are. No person can come to Christ unless he or she first recognizes a desperate need. One thing we know about this Canaanite woman is that she recognized her need. When Jesus finally speaks to her, notice His words: "It is not right to take the children's bread and toss it to their dogs" (v. 26).

Remember, Jesus is the Bread of Life and Jews are the Children of God. The Jews called the Gentiles "dogs." It may seem cruel for Jesus to allude to the woman as a "dog." But notice how she accepts the designation. She is not asking for a place at the table; she only asks for a crumb that might fall on the floor.

Often we come to God asking for a blessing, but we come with our pride and we leave unblessed. Worshippers often vacate the assemblies of the church unblessed because they cling to their own likes and dislikes: the way we like to do things; the way we like to hear things; the way we like to sing things. We leave unblessed and we wonder why. The words of the great Christian hymn must first apply to ourselves: "Nothing in my hand I bring. Simply to thy cross I cling."

Also Jesus is silent here *to reveal something to us about who He is.* New paganism in the church today expresses itself through attitudes such as: "God has to save me! I mean, I've been baptized, haven't I?" The cynic Voltaire said concerning God's forgiveness ". . . it's His job." But in reality God has saved us by His own choice. It is neither His obligation nor His duty. Salvation is certainly at the discretion of God.

The silence of God should wake us up to this reality. How we take God for granted! Thielicke said, "And I make bold to say that even the most orthodox churchman will not enter the kingdom of heaven unless he is continually surprised that mercy has been shown him."[2] God doesn't force His mercy upon us. It was not Christ's duty to die for us. Perhaps it is when grace ceased to be amazing to us that we cease to be under grace.

Third, the silence of God is *His greatest test of faith*. What would you have done had you been this woman? Notice how she responds. She "came to him, crying out, 'Lord, Son of David, have mercy on me! My daughter is suffering terribly from demon-possession' " (Matthew 15:22). And then "she keeps crying out" (v. 23) after them. Then she kneels before Him and begs Him " 'Lord, help me!' " (v. 25). Finally, conceding to His description of her as a dog, she says, " 'Yes, Lord, . . . but even the dogs eat the crumbs that fall from their masters' table' " (v. 27).

Martin Luther said concerning this story: "She catches him in his own words." Maclaren says: "She has flung the sack of his promises at his feet and he cannot step over it." You see, when you survive the silence of God, you can survive anything—the wind of persecution, the rejection of friends, the attacks of Satan. It's a test of faith.

But another reason here for the silence of Jesus is that He is using an enacted parable to teach His disciples about *the sickness to which creedal traditions can lead*. This chapter begins with some Pharisees and teachers of the law coming to Jesus and asking, " 'Why do your disciples break the tradition of the elders? They don't wash their hands before they eat!' " (v. 2). Jesus replied typically by asking them a question, "And why do you break the command of God for the sake of your tradition?" (v. 3).

In verse 6 He accused them of nullifying the word of God for the sake of their tradition. In verse 11 He teaches them that it's not what goes into a man's mouth that makes him unclean, but what comes out of his mouth.

The traditions of the elders had led Israel into a kind of exclusivism accompanied by a spiritual arrogance

---

"AND I MAKE BOLD TO SAY THAT EVEN THE MOST ORTHODOX CHURCHMAN WILL NOT ENTER THE KINGDOM OF HEAVEN UNLESS HE IS CONTINUALLY SURPRISED THAT MERCY HAS BEEN SHOWN HIM."

---

that said, "We're the only people who are right," and a lack of evangelistic concern that implied, "We're the only people who are right and we're glad it's that way; in fact, we sort of want to keep it that way."

Jesus moves His lectern from Israel out to the real classroom of life. Creedal traditions breed a false security. It's fairly easy inside these walls to say, "Everyone else is going to hell but us," and then to sit back and do nothing. But it's an entirely different matter to look into the eyes of the desperate unsaved and really see them. It's a different matter to look into the eyes of pain and to confront the real agony of the outside world. The traditions no longer make sense when they painlessly write off people.

No wonder His disciples were nervous. It was easy back in Israel to act sanctimonious toward the Gentiles. It was easy to call them "dogs." But it's not so easy for us to write them off when we look into their pleading eyes and hear their desperate cries. This is the only recorded time that Jesus took His disciples outside the borders of Israel. These are the men who will return to establish the churches for these unclean Gentile dogs.

Then Jesus heals the woman's daughter and the story is finished as quickly as it began. In verse 28, Jesus says to this persistent mother, "Woman, you have great faith!" In the original the "you" is emphatic. It was as if He were saying, "You may be a Gentile, but in comparison to these Israelites *you* have great faith." The disciples have learned a valuable lesson.

The chapter concludes with a striking contrast. Jesus goes back to Galilee. The crowds rush Him again. Large numbers are healed, almost without asking. This poor Gentile woman had to beg for a crumb. These Jews were given the Bread of Life freely. But now, because of her, the disciples are on their way to becoming world evangelists.

THINK TIME

1. What is Jesus trying to accomplish in this situation?
2. What lesson did the disciples learn?
3. How does it apply to us?
4. What are some ways God has been silent in your life?

5. What may be the purpose of that silence?
6. Compare the Jew-Gentile situation with the Christian-non-Christian situation of today.

[1]Helmut Thielicke, *A Thielicke Trilogy* (Grand Rapids: Baker Book House, 1980). p. 238.
[2]Ibid., p. 125.

MARK 10:46-52

Then they came to Jericho. As Jesus and his disciples, together with a large crowd, were leaving the city, a blind man, Bartimaeus (that is, the Son of Timaeus), was sitting by the roadside begging. When he heard that it was Jesus of Nazareth, he began to shout, "Jesus, Son of David, have mercy on me!"

Many rebuked him and told him to be quiet, but he shouted all the more, "Son of David, have mercy on me!"

Jesus stopped and said, "Call him."

So they called to the blind man, "Cheer up! On your feet! He's calling you." Throwing his cloak aside, he jumped to his feet and came to Jesus.

"What do you want me to do for you?" Jesus asked him.

The blind man said, "Rabbi, I want to see."

"Go," said Jesus, "your faith has healed you." Immediately he received his sight and followed Jesus along the road.

7

When God Is Still

Mark 10:46-52

"Jesus stopped and said, 'Call him' " (v. 49).

The first word I learned in the Tamil language was "po." It's a strong word in India. It means "Leave me!" or "Get out of here!" It is a word reserved for persistent beggars.

Most people find it very uncomfortable to be around beggars. In India they often swarm around white people, crying, touching, showing you their children. Beggars are always a pathetic sight.

In Mark 10:46-52 we read about a time when, in the middle of a very busy day, Jesus was confronted by a beggar and stopped to attend to his needs. In this story is a great lesson for each of us about the beggar and about the God who stopped for the beggar. It is also a lesson about ourselves and the wonderful way we come to faith.

Do you ever feel God is too busy for you? This lesson may have your name on it.

THE BEGGAR WHO STOPPED GOD

It was bad enough to be a beggar but our text says he was also blind (v. 46). Bartimaeus could not see the light. How we take our ability to see for granted! What would it be like never to see sunshine? What would it be like never to see moonlight? Or never to see color—the green grass, the blue sky? Or never to see the faces of those you love? Or to drink in the smiles of your children? Or to look into the eyes of your mother?

What would it be like to be unable to see approaching danger? Think of the insecurity! Think of the loneliness! But soon the Light of the World would be passing Bartimaeus' way. And he wanted to see.

The text implies that he was extremely poor (v. 46); he was sitting by the roadside begging. It was bad enough to be blind, but a blind person in a wealthy family would at least have some advantages: the comforts of a nice home, a helper perhaps, the security

---

THERE IS A TIME FOR SILENCE, BUT IT IS NOT WHEN WE ARE STANDING IN FRONT OF A BEGGING WORLD.

---

of material things, and food to eat. To be blind and indigent would cause one to have a feeling of total helplessness and hopelessness. No light! No bread! But Bartimaeus is about to be suddenly and unexpectedly in the presence of the Light of the World and the Bread of Life.

This man is blind and poor, yet he is a man of great faith. He has faith in the fact that Jesus can completely change his life for the better.

You can't help but wonder how it was that this beggar came to faith. He couldn't see, so he hadn't seen any of the miracles of Jesus.

People come to faith in different ways; some people by their own private study of the scriptures. When I preach on the subject of faith, I often get the urge to stop in the middle of the sermon and ask people to tell their own story of how they began to have faith in Jesus.

No doubt Bartimaeus had come to faith by hearing other people talk about Jesus. He certainly hadn't been sitting around studying the scriptures. He must have been excited by the testimonies of others whose lives had been changed by the Master; people who could say, even before the words of the song were written, "Once I was blind, but now I see."

I wonder why we don't talk about Jesus more. People can be identified by the things they like to talk about. For the most part, I don't hear Christian people talk much about Jesus except in rather formal settings designated for that purpose.

I really don't quite understand that! We talk politics; we gossip; we talk religion, hobbies, and sports . . . but not much about Jesus. Many churches today have become so afraid of Pentecostalism that anyone caught talking about Jesus outside of a duly ordained worship service is labeled "charismatic." But I really wonder which is worse: to go overboard or to be underenthusiastic?

Maybe this would be the key to starting an evangelistic renewal. If we could just get our people to start talking about Jesus! On the job! At school! Around the dinner table! At the office! In the factory! We should be able to talk about Jesus as we would a family member or a dear friend. To the Christian Jesus should be both, so why should it be so uncomfortable to talk about Him?

This beggar would have never been saved from his blindness had he not heard someone talking about

---

HE HAD A LOST WORLD TO THINK ABOUT. HE WAS ABOUT TO MAKE ATONEMENT FOR A FALLEN RACE. BUT HE STOPPED IN HIS TRACKS AND STOOD STILL FOR ONE PERSON.

Jesus. I wonder how many people could be reached for God today if all of us started speaking more about Jesus. If our deafness to the meaning of the words in the great old Christian song "You Never Mentioned Him to Me" were healed, then a great many blind beggars around us could be healed.

Maybe the first healing that needs to occur today is that of Christians who are deaf to the word and dumb to the world. There is a time for silence, but it is not when we are standing in front of a begging world. Someone has said that "many Christians are like arctic rivers. They are frozen at the mouth."

Not only is this beggar blind and poor, he is also desperate. He was so persistent in his appeal that he stopped Christ in His tracks. Over the buzz of the noisy procession, the shouting, the laughter, the bleating of Passover sheep, Jesus heard the piercing cry of a desperate beggar who wanted to be saved of his blindness. " 'Jesus, Son of David, have mercy on me!' Many rebuked him and told him to be quiet, but he shouted all the more, 'Son of David, have mercy on me!' " (vv. 47,48).

What does all this mean! Desperation can often give birth to a passionate commitment. People who are spiritually blind and desperate for the Light and people who are spiritually impoverished and desperate for the Bread can have it if they are willing to "go for it" in Jesus. Jesus is willing to stop and stand still in front of the poorest, most wretched person on earth. Jesus is willing to stop for us as individuals, stand still in front of us, and heal us.

THE GOD WHO STOPPED FOR THE BEGGAR

Now that we've considered the beggar, let's consider his Savior. Jesus was on His way to Jerusalem. He had another seventeen miles to go. Passover was just a few days away, and this Passover would be different. This year the Lamb of God would be sacrificed.

Talk about pressure! Nobody else has ever felt the pressure exerted upon Jesus during this last journey to Jerusalem. He made His way to the Holy City. He had a job to do—a terrible job. Soon, by His death, He would pay for the sins of the people. Everywhere small processions of people were making their way to Jerusalem, many of them carrying their own little lamb for the annual sacrifice. But moving now through Jericho, rapidly, the Lamb of God was on His way to His destiny—the eternal sacrifice.

Jericho was a beautiful city, called by some the Garden of Eden in Israel. Thielicke said it was "noted for its palms and notorious for its snakes." Jesus was in the new Jericho. The old ruins were just up the road. Old Jericho had been destroyed some fourteen hundred years earlier. In 1929, Dr. John Garstangt excavated these old ruins and confirmed that the walls did fall flat just as described in Joshua 6. New Jericho was built southwest of these ruins.

Jesus was now moving through Jerusalem toward the climax of His redemptive mission. In the same verse (v. 46) Jesus enters and departs the city. The implication is clear. Jesus is on the move. Nothing can stop Him now. But then—something (or rather, someone) did.

"Jesus, Son of David, have mercy on me!" (v. 47). And the text says "Jesus stopped" (v. 49). Jesus always took time to stop for a cry of desperation. God stopped! He stood still because of a blind beggar's desperate cry.

Not many blind beggars are around us today, are they? But everywhere is desperation—jobs lost, marriages lost, purity lost, children lost, families estranged, friends hurt. Desperation stopped God! And it still can. Fourteen hundred years earlier, Joshua, not far from this very spot, stopped the sun in the sky. This blind beggar stopped the Son of God in His tracks.

An old saying goes, "When you're there, be all there." And Jesus was all there. For a moment, thoughts of the cross were put aside and Jesus made Himself fully available to the beggar. For a moment, thoughts of His redemptive suffering were gone. He was all there for a single desperate man. He had a lost world to think about. He was about to make atonement for a fallen race. But He stopped in His tracks and stood still for one person.

I am sometimes inclined to think that God is too busy for me. Then I think of the beggar who stopped God. Here is proof that our God will stop everything and stand still for the lowliest human being on earth.

Then Jesus healed him. In a flash the beggar's blindness exploded in light and he saw the grass; not just the grass, but the green grass. He saw the sky; not just the sky, but the blue sky. Looking around he saw

---

SOMETHING TERRIBLE SETS INTO THE LIFE OF SOME CHRISTIANS WHO HAVE BEEN IN THE CHURCH FOR YEARS. IT'S CALLED ROUTINE. IT'S CALLED BLIND-NESS. AND IT'S A DESPERATE SITUATION.

---

the smiling and amazed faces of people in the crowd. The procession began to move on, and naturally the man followed Jesus.

Now think of the excitement in that little band of followers. Think of the things they must have talked about during those last few miles to Jerusalem. Something is exciting about being in a place where Jesus is working. That's the way every church service ought to be—because Jesus is still working!

Well, who is this story for? It's for blind people who need the Light of the World. It's for hungry people who need the Bread of Life. It's for desperate people who need God to stop everything else to be all there for them.

It's for people who feel so low and indigent that they think no one cares.

But it's also for someone else. It's for people who once could see, but now are blind. The verb in verse 51 is *anablepo*. It can literally mean "to see again." W. E. Vine in his *Expository Dictionary of New Testament Words* indicated that perhaps there was a time when Bartimaeus could see.[1] Now he wanted to see again.

I wonder how many Christians grow blind after years of seeing, how many hearts grow hard and how many eyes are clouded by spiritual cataracts. Sensitivity is gone! Excitement is gone! First love is gone! Something terrible sets into the life of some Christians who have been in the church for years. It's called routine. It's called blindness. And it's a desperate situation.

But like the beggar—

You can be healed—

When you come to Jesus!

THINK TIME

1. How persistent are you with God?
2. How persistent do you think God wants us to be with Him?
3. How often do you talk about Jesus?
4. Do you feel comfortable talking about Jesus?
5. Has he healed any weaknesses in your life?

[1]W. E. Vine, *Expository Dictionary of New Testament Words* (Old Tappan, N. J.: Fleming H. Revell Company, 1966.), p. 29, addenda.

MATTHEW 18:1-14

At that time the disciples came to Jesus and asked, "Who is the greatest in the kingdom of heaven?"

He called a little child and had him stand among them. And he said: "I tell you the truth, unless you change and become like little children, you will never enter the kingdom of heaven. Therefore, whoever humbles himself like this child is the greatest in the kingdom of heaven.

"And whoever welcomes a little child like this in my name welcomes me. But if anyone causes one of these little ones who believe in me to sin, it would be better for him to have a large millstone hung around his neck and to be drowned in the depths of the sea.

"Woe to the world because of the things that cause people to sin! Such things must come, but woe to the man through whom they come! If your hand or your foot causes you to sin, cut it off and throw it away. It is better for you to enter life maimed or crippled than to have two hands or two feet and be thrown into eternal fire. And if your eye causes you to sin, gouge it out and throw it away. It is better for you to enter life with one eye than to have two eyes and be thrown into the fire of hell.

"See that you do not look down on one of these little ones. For I tell you that their angels in heaven always see the face of my Father in heaven.

"What do you think? If a man owns a hundred sheep, and one of them wanders away, will he not leave the ninety-nine on the hills and go to look for the one that wandered off? And if he finds it, I tell you the truth, he is happier about that one sheep than about the ninety-nine that did not wander off. In the same way your Father in heaven is not willing that any of these little ones should be lost."

8

How Should I Act Anyway?

Matthew 18:1-14

"He called a little child and had him stand
among them" (v. 2).

*H*ave you ever been in an uncomfortable
situation where you did not know how to act? An
interesting story about President Calvin Coolidge amply
illustrates the point. He had invited two gentlemen to
a dinner party at the White House, neither of whom
were accustomed to such a great honor.

Very nervous about the whole situation, they agreed
between them that they would watch the President and
do whatever he did. When after-dinner coffee was
brought to the table the President took his cup and
poured about half the contents into his saucer. His two
guests did the same. Coolidge then poured into the
saucer a rather large quantity of cream. The gentlemen
followed suit. The President blew gently over this cream
and coffee mixture. So did the men. Then the President
put his saucer on the floor for the cat!

I can identify with that situation. Certain people and
certain scenarios tend to make me uncomfortable and
affect my behavior. It's funny how we sometimes tense

up around some personality types and not around others. Our behavior often changes a bit depending upon the people in our presence.

So, how are we supposed to act anyway? Are some personality traits to be especially desired and some to be rejected. Does some kind of standard give us a clue concerning what personality characteristics are to be desired?

The answer, of course, is yes, and the source is Jesus. In an age of relativity and tolerance we have found ourselves trying to be open to other lifestyles and behavioral characteristics. Often we have felt so unsure

---

CHILDISHNESS CAN BE SEEN IN MANY WAYS IN TODAY'S CHURCHES AND IS MOST OFTEN EXPRESSED BY THE ATTITUDE: "I'M GOING TO GET MY WAY, OR I'M GOING TO A DIFFERENT CHURCH."

---

about how to act that we have simply opted to drop out. Often a lack of shepherding has existed in our congregations because church leaders have lacked the confidence to take stands on various personality issues.

But why should we be quick to make a distinction between spiritual personality disorders and doctrinal disorders? Jesus made it quite clear that certain personality traits are not only to be desired but also to be demanded for the kingdom's sake. Many churches would find themselves in a more positive growth pattern if stands were taken not only on so-called doctrinal issues but more guidance was given in helping individuals know what kind of personality God wants them to have.

For too long now we've heard people say, "Well, that's just the way I am; I've always been this way and that's the way I'll always be." For too long we've heard people (even church leaders) say the same thing in order to overlook a particular problem: "Ah, that's just the way he is."

If this is just a matter of being patient while a person grows in the Lord, that's one thing. But when it becomes a diversion enabling us to escape our responsibility to each other, that's a different story all together. The fact is the Lord was very specific about some of the personality traits we should grow into.

HUMILITY

"He called a little child and had him stand among them. And he said: 'I tell you the truth, unless you change and become like little children, you will never enter the kingdom of heaven' " (v. 2,3). One tradition tells us that the child Jesus singled out was Ignatius of Antioch, who later became a great church leader and martyr. Ignatius' surname was Theophoros, which means "God-carried."

Of course we cannot know for sure which child it was, but what an impression it must have made on that child for the rest of his life! Think of the stories he could have told his grandchildren. And think of the emotions that person must have felt every time this Scripture was read!

Jesus is very definite about the fact that his followers are to be childlike. It's important to notice that Jesus said childlike and not childish, for a vast difference exists between the two.

Childishness is best represented by self-centeredness. Obsession with self is a trademark of our age. Numerous books and articles have chronicled the last quarter of the twentieth century as an age of narcissism. Narcissism is an immature preoccupation with self. The term comes from the legend of Narcissus, a beautiful Greek youth who one day became so enamored with his own reflection in a river that he stayed on the bank, gazing at himself until he actually sprouted roots and turned into a flower.

The spirit of self-centeredness has produced in our age an unprecedented epidemic of loneliness, alcohol and drug abuse in record-breaking proportions, legions of babies born out of wedlock, skyrocketing rates of teen-age promiscuity, a holocaust of abortions, massive divorce rates, hideous child abuse statistics and other social problems.

Childishness can be seen in many ways in today's churches and is most often expressed by the attitude that: "I'm going to get my way, or I'm going to a different church." Many communities have developed an unhealthy competition among congregations, which not only fosters this kind of childishness but also tends to produce it.

Childlikeness is best characterized by attitudes that are outwardly directed in a positive manner. One such characteristic is dependence. A child is totally dependent upon his or her parents. While many psychologists are encouraging us to become autonomous, independent and self-actualized, Jesus is telling us that we need to learn to depend upon the Heavenly Father. Related words are *reliance, faith, trust* and others.

RESPONSIBILITY

"But if anyone causes one of these little ones who believe in me to sin, it would be better for him to have a large millstone hung around his neck and to be drowned in the depths of the sea" (v. 5-7).

The term "little child" had a double meaning to first-century readers. Naturally it could have been taken literally and understood to be a small child. The term could also mean a "young disciple" or a "new convert." Most probably the selection for this context would be a new Christian.

We are responsible for each other. We are our brothers' keepers. Church families today need to take this admonition seriously. Jesus goes on to show exactly how serious this responsibility is.

A person who damages the faith of a new convert is in jeopardy. Jesus said it would be better for him to be drowned in the sea.

Drowning was a Roman punishment, for the most part not used by the Jews as a form of capital punishment. It was considered a far too hideous way to die. The Jews were very frightened of the sea. Josephus mentions a terrible time in Jewish history during a Galilean revolt when angry Jews took the supporters of Herod out to the middle of the lake and drowned them. This represented to them utter annihilation.

Jesus shows us here just how serious a matter it is for Christians to be responsible for each other. The key word here is the word *sin*. Sin is not to be taken lightly. We are to help each other keep from sin. Under no circumstance are we ever to encourage sin. While it has its tantalizing powers, it is not something for the Christian to play around with.

Marriages break up because of sin. Families fall apart because of sin. Children are neglected because of sin. Churches split because of sin. Hearts are broken because of sin. Bodies are abused because of sin. Relationships are shattered because of sin. People go to hell because of sin. The devil rejoices because of sin. Jesus went to the cross because of sin. Sin is not to be taken lightly.

Yet, today's culture has been successful in desensitizing us to sin's power. The humor of the world causes us to laugh. The drama of the world entertains us. The value system of the world allures us. It's hard to hate sin when you're being entertained by it. But preaching against it certainly brings out the anger in church members who have acquired the sophistication of the world.

The mission principle called "identification" states basically that, to reach a culture, one must identify with it and go in "on its side." Naturally, to a certain extent, this is true. But when Christians try so hard to identify with the culture that they can't be distinguished from the culture's participants something is wrong.

Jesus did not come for the exclusive purpose of identifying with the culture. A certain amount of identification was involved with His ministry. He came as a human being. He lived in the same manner as His countrymen and for the most part participated in their customs and traditions. But that's where the similarities ended. From that point on, the mission of Jesus was strictly countercultural. And so it should be with ours.

We are to be responsible for each other. Church shepherds should particularly take this admonition to heart. But the command to be responsible for each other is not just for church leaders. It's for every Christian.

"If your hand or your foot causes you to sin, cut it off and throw it away" (v. 8). Because sin is so terrible, the Christian should constantly be involved in self-examination. When sin enters one's life, it becomes necessary to go to any viable length to remove it. It's better to do that than to be thrown into an eternal fire.

THE VALUE SYSTEM OF THE WORLD ALLURES US. IT'S HARD TO HATE SIN WHEN YOU'RE BEING ENTERTAINED BY IT.

The eternal fire that Jesus is talking about here is Gehenna, or the Valley of Hinnom. Students of Old Testament history will remember that it was at this valley that renegade Jews sacrificed their children to Moloch. In the days of Jesus it was a continuous incinerator.

As true as this application is for the individual Christian, it is even more applicable to the church as a congregation. Only three times is it recorded that Jesus ever mentioned the word *church:* once in Matthew 16:18 and twice in Matthew 18:17. Of course He alluded to it in many different ways, but only three times is it recorded that He used the specific word *church*.

I believe that Jesus' intent here was to admonish His disciples to keep the coming church pure. Jesus does not want anyone to perish, but He certainly doesn't want to lose an entire congregation because of the sins of a few who will not change. The good of the majority must not be imperiled by the rebelliousness of a minority.

SENSITIVITY

"If a man owns a hundred sheep, and one of them wanders away, will he not leave the ninety-nine on the hills and go to look for the one that wandered off? And if he finds it, I tell you the truth, he is happier about that one sheep than about the ninety-nine that did not wander off" (v. 12,13).

It's alright to be upset when someone else has a problem. It's alright to rejoice when someone gets a problem worked out. The idea of hiding our emotions is not rooted in biblical teaching, but in a machismo philosophy of life.

In the days of Jesus, Palestinian shepherds were highly skilled in taking care of their flocks. Their work required an extreme amount of dedication and often a considerable degree of sacrifice. When the going got tough, the work required an extraordinary amount of sensitivity for the sheep. A person who lacked patience would certainly not be suited for the job. Sheep are some of the most unintelligent animals on four legs.

No amount of energy was spared when it came to tracking down a lost sheep. William Barclay maintains it was a rule that if a sheep could not be brought back alive, at least the fleece or carcass would be brought back to explain how the sheep had died. The shepherd's dedication in this strenuous pursuit often brought him into dangerous situations.

So who is the shepherd? Of course the Bible teaches that the Chief Shepherd is Jesus Christ (see 1 Peter 5:4). The idea of God the Father as a Shepherd also has biblical precedence (see Genesis 48:15). God pursues us when we go astray. He is sensitive to our needs as well as our tendencies. He is determined not to let us leave the fold easily.

In the New Testament Church, elders were also called shepherds (see 1 Peter 5:2). Elders are to be tenacious about keeping their flock safe and healthy. They are to love each sheep with an individual love and must be prepared to go to any length to rescue a sheep in danger.

One of the most frightening passages in the entire Bible is where God speaks to his Old Testament elder-shepherds and accuses them of being unfaithful to the flock.

"Therefore, you shepherds, hear the word of the Lord: As surely as I live, declares the Sovereign Lord, because my flock lacks a shepherd and so has been plundered and has become food for all the wild animals, and because my shepherds did not search for my flock but cared for themselves rather than for my flock, therefore, O shepherds, hear the word of the Lord: This is what the Sovereign Lord says: I am against the shepherds and will hold them accountable for my flock" (Ezekiel 34:7-10).

But in a very real sense, every Christian can be considered a shepherd. We all have our own spheres of influence. They may be our families, Sunday school classes or friendship groups. Every Christian needs to take seriously the admonition to be a totally determined shepherd. I can think of no factor that would usher in a new age in our churches more rapidly than if we were to all follow the Lord's will in this matter.

But it will require a sensitivity to one another's needs. Beyond the feelings themselves, it will require a willingness to go to any length to meet the spiritual needs of our flocks.

So how am I supposed to act? I want to have the kind of personality that the Lord wants me to have. I know that He grants me some areas as part of my own individuality. But I also know that He wants me to have some specific personality traits. If I do not have them, He wants me to be growing in these areas. To be humble; to be respectful; to be sensitive—there is no doubt as to God's will for these traits to be in my life.

THINK TIME

1. What characteristics of a child would not be appropriate for Christian living?
2. What childlike characteristics would be desirable?
3. By your influence, whom in your circle of acquaintances could you introduce to Christ?
4. What is the difference between being childlike and childish?
5. Think about your own personality characteristics.

LUKE 19:29-44

After Jesus had said this, he went on ahead, going up to Jerusalem. As he approached Bethphage and Bethany at the hill called the Mount of Olives, he sent two of his disciples, saying to them, "Go to the village ahead of you, and as you enter it, you will find a colt tied there, which no one has ever ridden. Untie it and bring it here. If anyone asks you, 'Why are you untying it?' tell them, 'The Lord needs it.' "

Those who were sent ahead went and found it just as he had told them. As they were untying the colt, its owners asked them, "Why are you untying the colt?"

They replied, "The Lord needs it."

They brought it to Jesus, threw their cloaks on the colt and put Jesus on it. As he went along, people spread their cloaks on the road.

When he came near the place where the road goes down the Mount of Olives, the whole crowd of disciples began joyfully to praise God in loud voices for all the miracles they had seen:

"Blessed is the king who comes in the name of the Lord!"

"Peace in heaven and glory in the highest!"

Some of the Pharisees in the crowd said to Jesus, "Teacher, rebuke your disciples!"

"I tell you," he replied, "If they keep quiet, the stones will cry out."

As he approached Jerusalem and saw the city, he wept over it. . . .

9

Following Through When The Going Gets Rough

Luke 19:28-44

*J*esus had just been to Jericho. He is now resolutely set for Jerusalem. It's only about seventeen miles from Jericho to Jerusalem. The road winds uphill through wilderness country most of the way. Though the geographic difference is slight, the theological difference is enormous. Had Jesus stayed in Jericho, there would have been no Jerusalem. Had there been no Jerusalem, there would have been no cross; no cross, no atonement, no atonement, no salvation. For all of us today, the distance between Jericho and Jerusalem is the difference between heaven and hell.

Jesus is not just on His way to Jerusalem. He is moving toward His destiny and the collective destiny of every human being who ever lived. He's making that trip for Adam, Moses, David, Paul, you, and me.

Each of us can learn from this final journey to Jerusalem. It's a lesson in how to follow through when the going gets tough.

Being an adjunct professor at a local university gives me an opportunity to work with quite a few ministerial students. One characteristic I notice among many students is the desire to jump into a particular task and then to lose heart and not go on to finish the work. Though I go to careful pains to point out the problem, it doesn't concern me a great deal because I realize that this tendency is a rather normal trait of immaturity. Nevertheless, it is a weakness that must be overcome if we are to become all that we were meant to be. As Jesus makes His way to Jerusalem, if we look closely, we can learn the lesson of how to finish the work God has given us to do.

RESOLUTION: KNOWING WHAT
I HAVE TO DO

Jesus had purposefully been staying out of Judea. He had a price on His head; the Jews wanted Him dead. He had become the most popular young preacher in all

---

EVERY CHRISTIAN HAS A JERUSALEM, IN FACT MANY JERUSALEMS, TO JOURNEY TO. A CULTURE OBSESSED WITH FINDING "SELFHOOD" HAS USED THE WRONG ROAD MAP.

---

of Israel. Jewish leaders were jealous. The religious establishment was filled with hatred because He was shaking so many of its time-honored traditions. As a result of His redemptive ministry, people all over the country were beginning to question the credibility of the

Jewish leaders; consequently, Jesus was targeted for elimination.

Jesus knew all this. Nevertheless, He was resolutely determined to finish His work (see Luke 9:51). His disciples had been advising Him against a return to the Holy City: ". . . a short while ago the Jews tried to stone you, and yet you are going back there?" (John 11:8). But because Jesus fully recognized the importance of His mission, He had the courage to walk right into the lion's den; right up to the chopping block.

By doing that, He set the stage for all who would follow Him. Jesus was determined to be faithful to His duty; His purpose; His mission. He was resolute in seeing the matter through.

What a lesson for us today! Duty is not a matter of option. Every Christian has a duty to perform—a duty that does not rest on a prerequisite of comfort or self-concern. That duty must be seen in terms of our mission and purpose. To stop at Jericho is to short-circuit the will of God for our lives.

Every Christian has a Jerusalem, in fact, many Jerusalems, to journey to. A culture obsessed with finding "selfhood" has used the wrong road map. In the long run, the proper understanding of our duty is what develops our inner "self." And the biblical view of self is that it is something to be *developed*, not *discovered*. A generation lost in the wilderness of "self-exploration" will not make it to the promised land of self-fulfillment. Their bones will bleach white in the nether land desert of Kadesh Barnea.

This principle can be applied to every aspect of our lives: marriage, parenting, business, education. Every area of our lives is accompanied by a Christian duty or mission. Any area devoid of this duty does not belong to a Christian lifestyle. When we know what we have to do and we see it in terms of our duty (mission) then follow-through becomes essential.

Immanuel Kant called this the Categorical Imperative. "Though the heavens fall," I will be true to my mission. Jesus was true to His mission. He did not linger in Jericho. He was determined to follow-through.

CONFIDENCE: KNOWING WHO I AM

"Blessed is the king who comes in the name of the Lord!" (v. 38). Over and over these shouts came from the people. As the King made His entry into the capital city, the people lined the streets, threw their cloaks down on the roadway to carpet His passage, and welcomed Him as a conquering hero. Jesus accepted their praise. But He knew full well that very soon those shouts of hosannas would be turned to shouts of "Crucify him! Crucify him!" (Luke 23:20).

Because Jesus knew who He was, He was able to finish the work. Because He was certain of His person, He was certain of His purpose. His entrance to Jerusalem was characterized by several interesting aspects.

First there was His *meekness*. Jesus is King of the Universe. "Through him all things were made; without him nothing was made that has been made" (John 1:3). "For by him all things were created" (Colossians 1:16).

But He rides into Jerusalem on a donkey. Conquering Pharaohs rode in stallion-drawn chariots. Alexander the Great and, later, the Caesars rode in on magnificent warhorses. Within just a few years General Titus will ride into this same city as conqueror. But Jesus enters His city as the King of Peace—riding on a donkey that belonged to someone else.

"Rejoice greatly, O Daughter of Zion! Shout, Daughter of Jerusalem? See, your king comes to you, righteous and having salvation, gentle and riding on a donkey, on a colt, the foal of a donkey. I will take away the chariots from Ephraim and the warhorses from Jerusalem, and the battle bow will be broken. He will proclaim peace to the nations" (Zechariah 9:9).

Jesus never forces Himself upon anyone! Unlike the leaders of Islam, who force people to accept their doctrines at the point of a sword, Jesus offers the freedom of choice—even rejection. Even in His omnipotence, Jesus chose to ensure the freedom of choice for His own creation. He comes into Jerusalem meekly.

Second, there was MISUNDERSTANDING. Those who were shouting loudest were among those who misunderstood most. They hailed Him as an earthly king. "Blessed is the king who comes in the name of the Lord!" (v. 38). "Hosanna," (John 12:13) is a one-word Hebrew prayer meaning "Lord, save us." They sought salvation from Rome. He offered salvation from sin.

The Gospel of John tells us that the people spread palm branches along His way (see John 12:13). I like the way Herbert Lockyer describes the scene. Writing about the palm tree, he said, "the tree reached the height of dignity when its branches were used to wave a jubilant welcome to Him who made the trees. Nature is no infidel but has ever been the friend and ally of her Creator. The star led the wise men to the place of His birth. The sea closed its hungry mouth when He walked on the billows. The winds and waves obeyed His voice. The sun veiled its face as He hung upon the cross in agony and shame."

How true! The earth shook in agony and grief when its creator died. But the people did not understand the magnitude of this one whom they hailed as an earthly king—a worldly solution to all their earthly problems.

Still today most people seek an earthly treatment to all worldly problems. This perhaps is one of the most succinct ways of describing secular humanism. The philosophy of humanism is that we can provide our own solutions from among ourselves; that one of our

---

UNTIL WE REALLY UNDERSTAND WHO WE ARE, WE SHALL NEVER REALLY BE ABLE TO GRASP THE IMPORTANCE OF WHAT WE ARE TO DO.

---

own can save us from our problems. Like these Jews of old, we still misunderstand.

In addition to misunderstanding a secular solution, they were also wrongly focused on the inside. The question: "What can you do for me?", when it stands alone, is inadequate. It represents an obsession with self, which is not only unhealthy, but if never outgrown, can be destructive.

Many Christians today come to Jesus that way and unfortunately stay that way. I distinctly remember a particular woman in India. As I drove into her village in my jeep, she rushed out from her hut, charging at me. She clutched her ragged sari saying, "I have been a Christian for three years and this is all I have received." That sounds pretty crass to us Westerners, doesn't it?

Of course, the reality is that we simply rephrase the statement to make it sound less wordly. "Sunday evening services just don't do anything for me." Our statement may be less materialistic but it is, nevertheless, representative of self-orientation. How we continue to misunderstand the mission of Jesus!

Jesus' entry into Jerusalem was also characterized by the fact that it was MOMENTARY. In the midst of the waving palms, Jesus could see the shadow of the cross. It is frightening to see how quickly a mob can be swayed. The shouts of praise would soon become shouts of condemnation.

Even today, many join His ranks and sing His praise only to desert Him when the wind brings in a different feeling. Basing our convictions on feelings, even about commitment in marriage, in church, in school, in work is not sufficient to help us make it to the finish. Feelings are definitely important, but they change day by day Commitment must be grounded in something far more solid.

Jesus knew who He was! Therefore, He understood the importance of His mission. Until we really understand who we are, we shall never really be able to grasp the importance of what we are to do. Jesus taught this lesson most dramatically in John 13 when He washed His disciples' feet. How could He perform a task so humble?

It fit in with His mission to change the hearts of men. Because it fit in with His mission, His own ego did not preclude even the most humble act. "Jesus knew that the Father had put all things under his power, and that he had come from God and was returning to God; so he got up from the meal, took off his outer clothing, and wrapped a towel around his waist" (John 13:3,4). When you know where you've come from and where you're headed, you have the inner resources (provided from above) to finish the task.

DIRECTION: KNOWING WHO HE IS

Jesus had a special relationship with the city of Jerusalem. As He passed under the palm trees of Bethany on the old main road to the city, He dispatched His disciples to obtain for Him a young donkey. It is on this animal that His disciples placed Him. He rode into His own city, not on a warhorse but on an animal of peace. One writer called it a "procession of lowly pomp" but, beside it, the grandest triumphs of aggressive war and unjust conquest sink into utter insignificance.

His route took Him through green fields and under shady trees up to the Mount of Olives. The road suddenly swept northward and the city which hitherto had been hidden by the shoulder of the hill burst into full view.

Jerusalem! City of ten thousand memories. Its "imperial mantle of proud towers" was once regarded as one of the wonders of the world. Shimmering under the radiance of Sunday morning, the early light blazed a reflection off marble pinnacles and gilded roofs. The sounds of business transactions in the marketplace, regiments marching in drill, hawkers shouting out their advertisement, and children playing with visiting friends and cousins who had come for the Passover could be heard. One could see the smoke of a legion of breakfast fires rising upward into the clear Judean sky. If the census were right, Jerusalem had swelled to a population of around two and one half million for this special holy day.

From His vantage point on the hill Jesus could see the temple; beyond that—Calvary. Looking back in time He remembered fifteen centuries of revolutions and sieges, surrenders, and famines, each followed by brief restoration.

It was in this very valley that David fled from Absalom (see 2 Samuel 15:23). It was here that Asa destroyed his mother's idols, the Asherah. Here Athaliah was executed. This was the city of the Kings, of Saul, of David, of Solomon.

And, looking ahead a few years, He could clearly see a Roman general named Titus encompassing the city with his legions and embarking on a methodic genocide of the Jews. Jesus could see a forest of crosses, the massacre of women and children, and blood running ankle-deep in the streets. He could see myriads of Jewish adults and children locked together by ropes and chains to be taken away to slave markets of foreign lands. The body count would total almost a million and Jesus could see it all; every single corpse.

He could hear the agonizing cries of a conquered people. He knew that a new city would be called Colonia Aelia Capitolina. No Jew would be allowed to enter the city. No wonder Jesus wept!

H. F. Lyte wrote:

> The Son of God in Tears
> The angels wandering see;
> Hast thou no wonder, oh, my soul
> He shed those tears for me.
> He wept that we might weep,
> Might weep for sin and shame.
> He wept to show his love for us
> And bid us love the same.
> Then tender be our hearts,
> Our eyes in sorrow dim,
> Till every tear, from every eye
> Is wiped away by him.[2]

Jesus then made the sad statement: "If you, even you, had only known on this day what would bring you peace—but now it is hidden from your eyes" (v. 42). These people welcomed Him as a new Caesar; they did not know that He came instead as Savior.

Many people today recognize Him as a good man, perhaps even a great teacher. But they simply don't know who He really is. These ancient Jews honored Him as an earthly conqueror, the heir to the throne room of Rome. He came for heavenly conciliation, the heir to the throne room of the universe. If they had only known.

They cheered Him for pebbles when He had gold to offer. They praised Him as a man, not realizing He was God. But if they had only known. If they had only known. They were His fans, His spectators, but He had come for disciples. If only they had known.

Surely there are no sadder words than "if we had only known." Accepting the true identity of Jesus is the key to the power to follow-through in every aspect of our lives. Jesus did not come to earth just to change our "sweet by and by." He came also to give meaning to our "nasty now and now."

THINK TIME

1. How is your "follow-through" for the Lord? Be specific.
2. What "follow-through" characteristics do you see in Jesus?
3. What are some characteristics of "self-orientation?"
4. What characterizes your main thought process? "What can I do for the Lord?" or "What can the Lord do for me?"
5. What was the mission of Jesus Christ?
6. What is your mission for the Lord?

[1]Herbert Lockyer, *Twin Truths of Scripture* (Grand Rapids: Baker Book House, 1973), p. 133.
[2]H. F. Lyte, *Poems*, in *The Speaker's Bible* ed. James and Edward Hastings (Grand Rapids: Baker Book House, 1971, reprint edition), Volume III, p. 221.

MARK 11:12-18

The next day as they were leaving Bethany, Jesus was hungry. Seeing in the distance a fig tree in leaf, he went to find out if it had any fruit. When he reached it, he found nothing but leaves, because it was not the season for figs. Then he said to the tree, "May no one ever eat fruit from you again." And his disciples heard him say it.

On reaching Jerusalem, Jesus entered the temple area and began driving out those who were buying and selling there. He overturned the tables of the money changers and the benches of those selling doves, and would not allow anyone to carry merchandise through the temple courts. And as he taught them, he said, "Is it not written: 'My house will be called a house of prayer for all nations?' But you have made it 'a den of robbers.' "

The chief priests and the teachers of the law heard this and began looking for a way to kill him, for they feared him because the whole crowd was amazed at his teaching.

10

When Jesus Went To A Homecoming

Mark 11:12-18

Passover in Jerusalem was the annual Jewish homecoming, a yearly reunion of Jews from all over the world. There would never be another Passover like the one described in Mark 11. Jesus was there. And whenever Jesus is present, one thing you can always count on is that things get exciting.

The two events that occur in this passage (the cursing of the fig tree and the cleansing of the Temple) are part of the same immediate context. They go together. As the two events merge, we find a lesson desperately needed by the church today. A leafless fig tree and a defiled temple may at first seem like foreign elements to Christians who make their home in a vastly different culture and time frame from this first-century Christ. But a closer investigation reveals that in reality, we're not so far removed.

JESUS IS UNPREDICTABLE

Perhaps the worst thing many Christians do to Jesus

is to confine Him strictly to history. We are safer that way. We sense more security in a historical Christ than in one who is our contemporary. But the real Jesus was a person of great unpredictability. When it came to the matter of getting the job done, the only thing His disciples could do was to stand back and watch.

Naturally, in terms of keeping His promises, Jesus is absolute. We can know for certain that when Jesus made a promise, it would be kept beyond any shadow of a doubt. But the adventure of the Christian life lies in the fact that when it comes to the details of how Jesus is going to get the job done, He is positively unpredictable.

Think about the cursing of a tree and the cleansing of the temple. Who could have predicted Jesus' actions? Which of His disciples could have guessed that Jesus would have had this in His mind to be used as a lesson plan they would never forget? The reality of the matter in Jesus' day was that His disciples could never figure out which move He was going to make next. The same is true today. But one of the great tragedies of the twentieth century is that many disciples think they have Jesus all figured out.

Who would have ever thought of God being born in a barn; coming to earth as a baby; requiring His every need to be fulfilled by imperfect human beings? The logic of God supersedes the logic of man. Who would have thought that the conqueror would come in a crib and become a carpenter and then go to the cross?

As you read through the Gospels, a picture of His unpredictability begins to emerge. Jesus sends His disciples into a village to bring back something for lunch. After a long, hot hike into town and back again

He reveals to them that He has food to eat that they know nothing about (see John 4:32). Jesus heals a man who is demonized and then sends the legion of demons into a herd of pigs standing nearby (Mark 5:13). How strange! How unpredictable! (Someone has called this the first case of deviled ham in the world.)

Now think of how many of our apprehensions are tied to the unpredictability of life. One large hotel chain capitalizes on this fear by advertising: "No surprises." If there's anything we are scared to death of, it's a surprise. Our most brilliant financial thinkers and some of our most powerful computers are dedicated to trying

---

PERHAPS THE WORST THING MANY CHRISTIANS DO TO JESUS IS TO CONFINE HIM STRICTLY TO HISTORY.

---

to predict the stock market. Everyday we listen to a TV weather forecast that is supposed to help us know whether or not we need an umbrella for the next morning. A legion of psychological tests is available to help us predict job suitability, academic ability, and marital compatability. We just don't like unpredictability.

It's the same in the arena of religion. We want everything in nice neat packages with no surprises. That's why many Christians have quit believing in the Holy Spirit (at least in practice). He adds an element of unpredictability to our lives that tends to destabilize us. A considerable amount of credible research substantiates the fact that when the reformers began to desupernaturalize Christianity the stage was set for the development of the evolutionary theories that gave birth to the secular environment in which we find ourselves today.

If we can just keep Christ in the past tense, we feel more comfortable. In His historical setting we can keep Him safe and keep ourselves secure. The problem with this approach to Jesus is that it robs us of the adventure of the Christian life and diminishes the level to which our faith can grow. No doubt it also limits the work Jesus will do in our lives (see Matthew 13:58).

The real fact was that His disciples never knew what He was going to do. They were always off their guard. It is in this state of mind that faith finds its most fertile soil.

Read the events in the Gospels. Jesus was the one who messed up graveyards. He terrified folks at funerals. Can you imagine going to a funeral with Jesus in the audience? I don't know whether I'd keep my eyes on the Lord or on the corpse, waiting for an eye to pop open. He made wine out of bath water, saved a thief on a cross, and forgave His own murderers.

The hands that made all the trees in the world were nailed to wood. The mouth that spoke into existence the streams and rivers was parched with thirst. The Giver of Life died—died on a cold stone—and then sat up. Unpredictable! It was in His unpredictability that He revealed His power.

No wonder most of our churches lack power. We've made Him so predictable. He'd preach our sermons, cheer for our team, use our logic, sing our songs, fit into our humor, and be on our side in the debates, or so we've come to think.

Emil Durkheim, one of the greatest sociologists in recent history, introduced us to the concept of "totemism." Part of this principle involves the idea that people tend to deify their own values. People often project their own value system into a code of ethics that binds them. Rather than being revealed from a transcendent source, these values are actually only inner representations of our own feelings.

Think of how we have done this with Jesus. In Japan I've seen pictures of Jesus with slanted eyes. In India I've seen pictures of Jesus with the Hindu caste mark on His forehead. This may sound strange to Western readers but, when you think about it, most of the pictures you see of Jesus in our culture make Him look like King James. Not only have we done this with our art, we've also done it with our actions. We're certain He'd act just like us.

JESUS IS UNSTOPPABLE

Jesus is simply not impressed with our leaves! He goes straight for the fruit. Jesus looks beneath the covering of our diversions and scrutinizes our hearts. He is not as concerned with our surface, our circumference, our periphery. He's concerned with our hearts. The leaves make a good showing, but beyond that, what?

The fig tree in this incident represents Israel. Israel had become a nation that was hyperconscious of its exterior but very careless about its interior.

Jesus is not satisfied with hypocrisy and pretense. The tree does not exist in order to produce leaves. The leaves exist for the purpose of helping the tree to do what it was intended to do: produce fruit. The fig leaves hid the real emptiness of the tree's life. It existed in a totally nonproductive mode, but covered its reality with a diversion of leaves. This was not the first time fig leaves were used to cover a shameful situation. In the very beginning, Adam and Eve "sewed together and made coverings for themselves" (Genesis 3:7).

And we still do it. We still have our diversions to hide our lack of productivity. "Lord, look at our contributions. Lord, look at the fact that we go to church three times a week. Look at all the committees we belong to." The reality is that Jesus looks under all that at the heart.

As good as all these things are, they can be diversions if they hide a nonproductive life. Buildings, universities, church programs, and committees exist for the church and not vice versa.

The church today, like ancient Israel, needs to learn the lesson of the cursed fig tree. It is possible for a brotherhood, a congregation, or an individual to be deceived by the leaves. "Lord, we've got the right five steps"; "Lord, look at our beautiful baptistry." Now don't misunderstand. Leaves are important for a healthy tree, but the purpose of the tree is to provide fruit.

It was right around this same time that Jesus was teaching His disciples what would happen to Christians who would not bear fruit. "I am the true vine, and my Father is the gardener. He cuts off every branch in me that bears no fruit . . ." (John 15:1-2).

In this same passage He refers to the kind of cleansing a Christian must constantly experience. "You are already clean because of the word I have spoken to you" (John 15:3). And then "If anyone does not remain in me, he is like a branch that is thrown away and withers"

114

(John 15:6). As in Mark 11, Jesus teaches about cleansing and cursing.

Notice that the very next thing that Jesus does is to go straight to the Jewish Temple (see Mark 11:15). Jesus is completely unstoppable. He's going straight for the heart of Judaism. The heart of the Jewish nation was dirty and needed cleansing. Jesus had just employed an enacted parable to teach His disciple that diversion to hide reality is evil (i.e. the cursing of the fig tree). Now He is using another object lesson to show them that what was needed in Israel was heart surgery (the cleansing of the Temple).

Don't forget! Each Christian is the Temple of the Holy Spirit. The lesson from all of this is that Christians can be involved in multitudes of good things that in reality only hide a dirty heart. Jesus wants to cleanse our temples.

Just as Jesus went straight for the Temple, He goes straight to our heart. The sad thing is that so many people prohibit His entry because of a hard heart. Religious people can stop Him with a hard heart (see Heb. 3:7-12). What do you think those merchants did when He left the Temple? No doubt they set their tables and booths back up and resumed business as usual.

What do you think many religious people do today? Jesus visits their hearts, overturns a few things, shakes up a few traditions. Give it a few hours, and it's back to business as usual. These people are open for business with the world again!

Dr. Evan O'Neill Kane, sixty-two-year-old chief surgeon at Kane Summitt Hospital in New York, was convinced that major surgery could be performed while the patient was under a local anesthetic. On Feb. 15,

1921, he performed surgery on himself under a local anesthetic, removing his own appendix.

Occasionally we need to operate on ourselves and do a little exploratory heart surgery. What's the condition of your heart? Does your temple need cleansing?

JESUS IS AMAZING

Mark makes an interesting comment about the reaction of the people in the immediate aftermath of the temple cleansing. "The chief priests and the teachers of the law heard this and began looking for a way to kill him, for they feared him, because the whole crowd was amazed at his teaching" (v. 18). The word *amazed* here is a strong word in the Greek. It means to be "exceedingly struck in the mind"; to be "astonished." Something tragic happens in the hearts of religious people when they cease to be "amazed" at Jesus.

I particularly like the wording Luke uses when he describes the reaction of the people to the cleansing of the Temple: "Every day he was teaching at the temple. But the chief priests, the teachers of the law and the leaders among the people were trying to kill him. Yet they could not find any way to do it, because all the people hung on his words" (Luke 19:47-48).

Just think! Many of the movers and shakers wanted to harm Jesus but they couldn't because the people hung on His words and were continually amazed. Could it be that the cause of Jesus has suffered much today because so many of His people have lost the attachment to His words and the wonder?

Perhaps this is the real secret to church growth and Christian fruit-bearing. But it's so simple it almost seems impossible. Recapturing a sense of "amazement" is indeed a matter for the heart! And maybe the temple needs to be cleansed first.

THINK TIME

1. What are some of the amazing things Christ has done in your life?
2. What is something you could do that would amaze Jesus?
3. How has Jesus worked unpredictably in your life?
4. What are your feelings about how the Holy Spirit works in your life?
5. What aspects of your "temple" need cleansing?
6. Why is it so hard to allow Jesus into our innermost temple?

MATTHEW 25:1-13

At that time the kingdom of heaven will be like ten virgins who took their lamps and went out to meet the bridegroom. Five of them were foolish and five were wise. The foolish ones took their lamps but did not take any oil with them. The wise, however, took oil in jars along with their lamps. The bridegroom was a long time in coming, and they all became drowsy and fell asleep.

At midnight the cry rang out: "Here's the bridegroom! Come out to meet him!" Then all the virgins woke up and trimmed their lamps. The foolish ones said to the wise, "Give us some of your oil; our lamps are going out."

"No," they replied, "there may not be enough for both us and you. Instead, go to those who sell oil and buy some for yourselves."

But while they were on their way to buy the oil, the bridegroom arrived. The virgins who were ready went in with him to the wedding banquet. And the door was shut.

Later the others also came. "Sir! Sir!" they said. "Open the door for us!"

But he replied, "I tell you the truth, I don't know you."

Therefore keep watch, because you do not know the day or the hour.

11

Making Religion Personal

Matthew 25:1-13

"The virgins who were ready went in with him to the wedding banquet. And the door was shut" (v. 10).

The woman who approached me one Sunday after the morning service was obviously irate. In my thinking, the assembly had been uplifting and spiritual. Our song leader had done his usual good job of getting our sleepy worshipers atuned to the things of the Spirit. The prayers had been heartfelt and the worshipers attentive.

But all of this had escaped at least one person. When the final amen had been said, she rushed to the foyer and demanded to know why it was that our congregation did not have a particular kind of program that had recently caught her interest. She said, "I don't understand why the church doesn't get more involved with . . . !"

I replied, "This church, I'm sure, will be glad to do it as soon as you volunteer for the job." She became even angrier and subsequently changed churches.

Through the years, I've had numerous encounters, some friendly, some not so friendly, with people who ask, "Why doesn't the church do this?" or "Why doesn't the church do that?" Generally, that's a very frustrating experience because most often the person making the suggestion is not interested in getting personally involved in the suggested program. I suppose they want the preacher to drop everything he's involved in and begin work on their pet project.

One man stormed into my office demanding a public apology for a phrase I had used in the pulpit. The phrase I had used was: "You either take Jesus as your personal Savior or you don't take Him at all."

He complained, "The *church* doesn't believe that." When I explained my feelings on this matter and tried to help him understand why I was unable to change, he changed—churches, that is.

Both these episodes point out a dangerous trend among some Christians to accept a heresy that I call "depersonalized religion." Depersonalized religion is an attempt to either blame the church for one's own spiritual problem, or depend entirely upon the church for one's salvation.

JESUS AND PERSONAL RESPONSIBILITY

It was customary in weddings of Jesus' day for bridesmaids to escort the groom to the house of the bride. They carried with them small oil lamps to provide both light and festive decoration. In this parable Jesus is teaching the lesson of personal religion.

The ten bridesmaids represent to us modern-day church members. They are all part of the wedding party. They were all respectful of the groom (who represents

Christ) but half of them thought they could get by on the good works of the other half. When the groom finally made his appearance at midnight, half the church members were unprepared. Our parable designates them as "foolish"; tragically, they are left behind.

Please pay special attention to the fact that not only are they church members in attendance, they have the right kind of lamps and they are wearing the right kind of garments. They are in their appointed places and have rehearsed their assignments. But their lamps aren't burning because they forgot to bring the fuel—the oil—that makes the light.

MUCH OF THE PROBLEM LIES WITH A SYSTEM THAT TEACHES FAITH IN THE SYSTEM ABOVE FAITH IN A "PERSONAL SAVIOR." WHEN THE SYSTEM BECOMES MORE IMPORTANT THAN THE GROOM, THEN IT IS NOT LONG BEFORE WE GET CARELESS ABOUT FILLING THE LAMPS. SO MANY CHRISTIANS TODAY ARE NOT SPIRIT-FILLED AND, AS SUCH, ARE EMPTY LAMPS WITH NO LIGHTS.

They were depending on the light of other church members to get them into the wedding feast. But when the groom made his appearance, he refused to allow them entry.

Each church member is required to possess his or her own energy source. Each church member is commanded to be the Light of the World. Depersonalized religion says: "I'm in the right group" (I go to the right church), "I've got the right lamp" (I have the right interpretation of the Bible), and "I'm wearing the right garments" (I am surrounded by the right trappings of religion).

What are you doing to get you into the wedding feast of the Lamb? This question is not meant to be a slap in the face of grace because, ultimately, we all depend upon the grace of God as made manifest in the atoning life and death of Jesus Christ. But having accepted the fact that his responsibility has been and is being fulfilled, whose responsibility is it now as to whether I make it to the wedding feast or not? Is it the responsibility of my group? Or is it my responsibility?

Much of the problem lies with a system that teaches faith in the system above faith in a "personal Savior." When the system becomes more important than the groom, then it is not long before we get careless about filling the lamps.

Do you think you are a Christian because you've completed the right steps and every Sunday engage in the right acts? Do you think you are a Christian because you meet in a building with the right name on the sign out front? Do you think the fact that you sing in one particular style and use certain names for your preacher make you pleasing to God? If we are interpreting this parable correctly, then you may be surprised to discover someday that, like the five foolish bridesmaids, you were in the right place, at the right time, doing the right thing, but with an empty lamp.

It's a terrifying thought! It scares me to think of the large fringe membership in most of our churches. People are in their place on Sunday morning, Sunday night, and Wednesday evening, but are not lights in the midnight sin of our communities, showing other people the Bridegroom. People's lights aren't shining, not because they don't have the right lamps, but because they have no fuel. These people ultimately will be excluded from the feast.

THE CHURCH AND PERSONAL
RESPONSIBILITY

Twenty years ago William Banowsky made an important point on the distinction between the group and the individual. "Does the group give the power to the individual or does the individual give the power to the group?"

He goes on to answer this question by using the illustration of democracy and communism. "Democracy, at least in theory, has raised aloft the banner of the individual; while Communism champions the cause of collectivism. The frightening fact is really that of the degree to which the two sides are similar. The labels notwithstanding, we are more like the Russians than we dare admit . . ."[1] Perhaps this has become particularly true in our churches.

To any extent that it is true, it is also very tragic. To believe that power can be exerted from our collectives (our congregations) apart from the real spiritual power of our individuals is a travesty upon the Scripture we are now considering, especially given the technological capacity of our churches today to dispense light. In this computer age of advanced communications capabilities, our churches enjoy better organization, more specialized equipment, and finer educational resources than ever before, but seemingly, less power in the world.

When Jesus said, "You are the light of the world," He was speaking to individual people and not to the crowd as a singular unit. Jesus did not come as a group, a family, or a nation. He came as a person and His ministry did not get lost in the corporate activity of His followers. The combined energy of the group cannot replace the spiritual energy of the individual members who make up the group.

In our churches we must regain the commitment to teach and preach personal responsibility of our individual members. This parable teaches us that it is possible to be part of a group that belongs to the Bridegroom but not part of the Bridegroom. Being a disciple means more than having the right doctrines. Certainly the doctrines are critical but by themselves mean nothing.

NASA has a term it uses to describe a situation of utmost importance. If a certain system or piece of equipment is so critical that its failure would necessitate the termination of the entire mission it is designated as "criticality one."

When the O-ring protection system failed on the space shuttle "Challenger," the mission reached "criticality one." No matter what mission a Christian may be involved in, no matter what equipment he may be using, no matter what building he may be worshipping in, if he has no oil in his lamp, he has arrived at "criticality one."

THE CHRISTIAN'S SOURCE OF OIL

So where do we get this energy source? If it is critical to maintain fully energized lamps at all times, then how do we do it?

In the Bible, oil is often symbolic of the Holy Spirit. When David was ordained to be the future king of Israel, Samuel took a horn of oil and anointed him and the Spirit of God came upon him from that day forward (see 1 Samuel 16:13). Other passages imply the same kind of relationship between oil and the Holy Spirit. Whether or not this specific symbolism was intended in this parable, I don't know, but one thing I do know is that the application is still the same for us. A church member who is not filled with the Holy Spirit is not ready for the Lord to come.

So many Christians today are not Spirit-filled and, as such, are empty lamps with no lights. God's Holy Spirit within us gives us the inner fuel to let our lights shine in this world of darkness. Being filled with the Holy Spirit is not simply an optional item for Christians who want to be more spiritual. Being filled with the Spirit is a direct commandment of God (Ephesians 5:18).

How is it that a Christian can become filled with the Holy Spirit? Perhaps we have been afraid to deal with that question because we have seen so many doctrinal abuses in this area. No doubt, the subject of the Holy Spirit has been dreadfully handled in many churches today. But is this any reason to exclude the doctrine from our churches? Think of it. Most of the literature written by Christians from our fellowship has been concerned with what the Holy Spirit does not do.

John 7:37-40 is the key to understanding how it is that one becomes filled with the Holy Spirit. "If anyone is thirsty, let him come to me and drink" (John 7:37). Maintaining a personal relationship with a personal Savior is the answer. And this must be renewed every day.

How tragic to be excluded from the wedding feast! This would be a sad case under any circumstance, but it would be hideously compound to grow up in a system that is close—but empty. The wedding feast of the Lamb is one occasion I want to make. May we all be prepared as we *Watch for the Lamb!*

THINK TIME

1. What is "depersonalized religion"?
2. How does it affect your life? How does it affect the church?
3. Upon what or whom are you depending for salvation?
4. What is your Christian energy source?
5. What more could you be doing to help make your faith more personal?
6. What are some of the characteristics of being "filled with the Spirit"?

[1]J.D. Thomas, ed., Great Preachers of Today: Sermons of William S. Banowsky (Abilene: Biblical Research Press, 1967), p. 52.

JOHN 20:19-22

On the evening of that first day of the week, when the disciples were together, with the doors locked for fear of the Jews, Jesus came and stood among them and said, "Peace be with you!" After he said this, he showed them his hands and side. The disciples were overjoyed when they saw the Lord. Again Jesus said, "Peace be with you! As the Father has sent me, I am sending you." And with that he breathed on them and said, "Receive the Holy Spirit."

12

The First Sunday Night Church Service

John 20:19-22

"On the evening of that first day of the week, when the disciples were together" (v. 19).

THE FIRST DAY OF THE WEEK

I guess I've been to a multitude of church services like the one described in verses 19-20. I have preached for some of them. Do you know the kind I'm talking about? Starting off like a meal of stale, cold leftovers, the service ended up like a feast fit for royalty. To these meetings were brought our own little sack lunches of insufficiency but somehow, during the course of it all, Jesus miraculously fed the multitudes by multiplying the bread.

I love Sunday services. I grew up loving Sunday services. My earliest remembrances are of my parents bundling me up and taking me off to church. Both the morning and the evening services have special attractions to me and each service is distinct in feeling from the other. A warmth finds its way into the evening service that is often crowded out of the morning service by sleepiness, hunger (not spiritual), and a necessity to expedite the worship (which, being interpreted, means we want to beat the Baptists to the cafeteria). At any rate, Sunday nights have always been very special to me.

The first Sunday night service was much like many I've experienced, at least from one standpoint. The disciples had gathered together without realizing what was about to happen, without any expectations of the possibilities. Aren't we like that? We come with fears, plans, or anxieties on our minds, but we often lack the expectation—the single expectation—God wants us to have. We lack the expectation that in just a few minutes we are going to be involved in a serious meeting with the Almighty.

But there the similarity ends. That first Sunday evening service was unique in many ways. These desperate disciples had no idea what was just about to happen to them. They had no idea that just around the corner was a vision as big as the world itself; that from this little hideout in Jerusalem a force was about to be unleashed that would set into motion the church of Jesus Christ! That church would challenge Rome itself! That church would exist until the end of time, though every other kingdom crumbled into nothingness.

This little service was the first of thousands upon thousands to come. It set the precedent for us to believe that any time disciples get together, great things can happen.

"WITH THE DOORS LOCKED FOR FEAR OF THE JEWS"

In that first service, the doors were locked. The worshipers were behind closed doors of fear. The same is true with many of our churches today. Many of our congregations are scared churches in a suffering world. The problem, as Vance Havner puts it, is "not so much the wolfishness of the wolf as it is the sheepishness of the Lord's sheep."[1]

The doors that lock us in are called fear and faithlessness. No other doors are so tightly locked as these. A world of lost men and women wait outside the doors hungry for the Bread of Life, thirsty for the Living Water that eternally satisfies, are denied access because of our fear.

For these despairing disciples in John 20, Pentecost has not yet come. Yet another seven weeks must pass before the Comforter arrives to fill them with courage and passion. For many of our congregations today, it is still "pre-Pentecost." The Spirit has not yet come in fullness.

So many of our church services are about as exciting as waiting in line at the grocery store. The doors are tightly shut. The members are unexpectant.

But then, for the disciples gathered that evening, something happened . . .

"JESUS CAME AND STOOD AMONG THEM"

Everything changed as of that spectacular moment. But then that's the way it has always been: everything changes when Jesus comes. Perhaps that's the problem with many of our services—maybe Jesus is not there. If disciples today are unexcited to come together into His presence, why should the Master trouble Himself to come into their midst?

THESE DESPERATE DISCIPLES HAD NO IDEA WHAT WAS JUST ABOUT TO HAPPEN TO THEM. THEY HAD NO IDEA THAT JUST AROUND THE CORNER WAS A VISION AS BIG AS THE WORLD ITSELF.

But Jesus came into these troubled disciples' midst and spoke to them: "Peace be with you!" (v.19,21). He blesses them with the double peace, as one writer notes, "the peace of God" (Philippians 4:7) and "peace with God" (Romans 5:1).

Again it is Vance Havner who insightfully points out that "peace with God" puts us on the road to heaven, and the "peace of God" guards our hearts on the trip.[2] The church of Jesus Christ is the original Peace Corps, for a world that is exploding in war, crime, and violence, that's no small matter. The disciples will need this double peace for the job they have ahead.

But then Jesus reveals His scars . . . two thousand Easters had not yet passed so as of John 20 the Resurrection had not yet become routine. "He showed them his hands and side" (v. 20). He wanted them to see His wounds. He wanted them to know that life goes on beyond the wounds; that triumph can spring from tragedy; that the new criterion in the kingdom would be to measure a person by scars instead of awards, diplomas, degrees, pedigrees, or whatever.

He wanted them to identify with Him—the crucified Christ. Like Paul who could say, "I have been crucified with Christ" (Galatians 2:20), or Peter who ended up on a cross, or every new disciple who must take up his cross, we today must realize that the scars become the measure of the new man; that a funeral must come before a new birth. Too many of us are like the immature, pre-Pentecost Peter who confessed Christ (see Matthew 16:16) and then six verses later denied the cross (see Matthew 16:22).

"THE DISCIPLES WERE OVERJOYED"

Here is the true characteristic of what a Sunday service is supposed to be—joyful. I believe in dignity, but when dignity starts turning into rigor mortis, something is dreadfully wrong.

It is not enough to just check in, do our five acts, check out, and pick up our hearts and minds on the way out. Joy is a matter of both the heart and the mind and comes from looking at the Lord. The time comes to take our eyes off the storm and fasten them relentlessly on Jesus. One of the greatest heresies in the twentieth-century church is that worship can occur apart from the heart as long as the right activities are performed. How tragic!

These early disciples had a message of joy. No wonder they were able to take it to the entire world! No wonder Christianity exploded in growth! That message of joy sprang from a resurrected Christ whose kingdom had come with power, bringing true peace. A

135

message which concerns itself with spreading only the rules of the kingdom will find itself impotent in meeting the needs of a desperate world. Knowing the rules without knowing the Ruler is like trying to be satisfied with eating the shadow of a ham sandwich. There's no satisfaction (and certainly no joy) in the shadow of a ham sandwich.

Then comes the commission . . .

"AS THE FATHER HAS SENT ME, I AM SENDING YOU"

Every Christian is commissioned; God's army has no non-commissioned troops. In the Lord's church, we don't need to get rid of the clergy system; we need to get rid of the laity system. Every disciple is a clergyman or clergywoman. Every member is called, commissioned, and sent out with a purpose. Designating evangelism as the exclusive job of the "professional staff" has put us into a self-destruct mode, especially since we have required the staff to minister *to* us and not *from* us.

"AND WITH THAT HE BREATHED ON THEM AND SAID, 'RECEIVE THE HOLY SPIRIT' "

One thing we need today in the church is a breath of fresh air! We need the breath of God, the precious Holy Spirit. We need to quit spending so much time talking about what the Holy Spirit does not do and get back to the Book and find out what He *does* do. We need to quit arguing about the Spirit and start experiencing the Spirit. Disciples without the Spirit will forever remain quaking behind locked doors, worrying about the world.

For a church hiding behind locked doors, we need . . .
To hear the voice of Jesus speaking peace . . .
To see His wounds . . .
To have a fresh experience with His Spirit!

Until then . . . the doors to the world will not spring open.

THINK TIME

1. Compare the first Sunday night service with a typical service at your church.
2. Discuss the concept of "locked door." How is it relevant to you as an individual and to the church you attend?
3. What might the church do to put excitement back into worshipping the Lord?
4. Do you feel the presence of Jesus in your personal life?
5. Why is the Holy Spirit vital in your life?
6. What attitudes under your control can help to bring you greater joy in your life?

[1]Vance Havner, *Why Not Just Be Christians* (Old Tappan, N.J.: Fleming H. Revell Company, 1974), p. 58.
[2]Ibid., p. 61.

LUKE 24:36-49

While they were still talking about this, Jesus himself stood among them and said to them, "Peace be with you."

They were startled and frightened, thinking they saw a ghost. He said to them, "Why are you troubled, and why do doubts rise in your minds? Look at my hands and my feet. It is I myself! Touch me and see; a ghost does not have flesh and bones, as you see I have."

When he had said this, he showed them his hands and feet. And while they still did not believe it because of joy and amazement, he asked them, "Do you have anything here to eat?" They gave him a piece of broiled fish, and he took it and ate it in their presence.

He said to them, "This is what I told you while I was still with you: Everything must be fulfilled that is written about me in the Law of Moses, the Prophets and the Psalms."

Then he opened their minds so they could understand the Scriptures. He told them, "This is what is written: The Christ will suffer and rise from the dead on the third day, and repentance and forgiveness of sins will be preached in his name to all nations, beginning at Jerusalem. You are witnesses of these things. I am going to send you what my Father has promised; but stay in the city until you have been clothed with power from on high."

13

Where Do We Go From Here?

Luke 24:36-49

"And repentance and forgiveness of sins will be
preached in his name to all nations, beginning at
Jerusalem" (v. 47).

Some months ago I was assigned this
particular text for a major lecture at a Christian college.
When I first began to study it, I wondered what in the
world I was going to do with it.

The more I meditated upon it, however, the more I
began to sense the incredible vastness of this passage.
It was an experience akin to arriving at a ski lodge long
after sunset and not really being aware of the landscape
around you. In the inky blackness of the night you have
an intuitive sense that a "hugeness" lies all around
you—a grandeur, a splendor bigger than everything
else. Then as the sun makes its way up and begins to
illuminate the steep cliffs, the jagged rocks, and the lofty
peaks, you begin to feel overwhelmed.

This passage overwhelms me. I cannot meet all its
demands. Among the theological gems taught in this
passage is a clear-cut doctrine of the mission of the
people of God, a prophecy of the power that would

come to the people of God, and a divine confirmation to the people about the power—the Resurrection.

CALLED FOR A PURPOSE

Beginning at Jerusalem, the people of God would be a commissioned people, called for a purpose—to penetrate all the cultures of this world with the story of Jesus (see v. 47). The commission to the church is to penetrate our communities with the Good News of the gospel. It is to develop strategies of penetration aimed at getting the Good News into our towns and cities.

Jesus came to seek and to save the lost. He did not come to debate the issues. He did not come to fight the brethren. He did not come to take sides with the culture. He did not come to take sides against the culture. He came to take over!

Our purpose as His churches in our various communities and cultures is not to sit back and just condemn the culture. Neither is it to make a peace treaty with the culture. Our job is to take over. Our job is to build strategies of evangelism that will enable us to penetrate, infiltrate, and contest our culture for the minds of men and women, boys and girls.

To do that we've got to understand something about the Zeitgeist; that is, the spirit of our age. Who is determining the values of our culture? Who is setting the standards? Is the church influencing those standards or is it, in fact, being influenced by them?

Jesus described Christians as the salt of the earth. The purpose of salt is to penetrate; until it does, it is virtually useless. After it penetrates it can fulfill its purpose of flavoring and preserving. What good is salt confined to its shaker? What good are Christians confined to their buildings? A building-oriented approach to our faith has almost proved disastrous. It is not that we should not have buildings, it is simply that they should not have us.

Our culture is largely shaped by an incredibly complicated force called the media. The old question of whether the media shapes the culture or the culture shapes the media has almost become a moot point. Unfortunately the impact of the media has done more to penetrate the mission of the church than vice versa.

Nearly a hundred years ago an almost prophetic voice from Denmark, that of Soren Kierkegaard, said, "Supposing someone someday were to invent a giant talking

---

JESUS CAME TO SEEK AND TO SAVE THE LOST. HE DID NOT COME TO DEBATE THE ISSUES.

---

tube by which he could address the entire populous at once; surely the police would have to arrest him lest the entire nation become deranged."[1] Ours is a culture gone crazy. The commission to the church is not to become a reflection of the culture, but rather to be a major influence shaping the culture. Unfortunately Johnny Carson has probably had more impact on the personalities of many "Christians" than Jesus Christ.

Let me remind you that Jesus came to make sweeping changes in the lives of individuals as well as in the forces that shape cultures. The commission He gave to us was not to preach to the culture but to bring it to repentance (see v. 47). To do that, Christians and churches must be willing to pay the price, both in terms of financial commitment and personal commitment. The old model of hiring a preacher to do the job for us has not worked and is, in fact, unworkable. Churches claiming to be New Testament churches must now return to the model given in the New Testament or prepare to face extinction.

The first lesson in this model is that the purpose of penetrating the culture is to bring people to repentance. The cultural seduction of the church has made us feel at ease with the tactics of this world. How can we find ourselves in a position where we are entertained by the same forces in the world that brought Jesus to the cross? The humor and romance of Zeitgeist has lulled us into a complacency that, unchecked, will prove fatal to the cause we have labeled New Testament Christianity.

Only a fresh look at Jesus can bring us back. At this point in our history the church is not so much in need of revival as resurrection. The great hope for us is that we have in our history the precedent for resurrection. The body of Christ came back from the dead once before. The Body of Christ (His Church) can do it again today.

CLOTHED WITH A POWER

Not only are we called for a purpose, but we are clothed with a power. "I am going to send you what my Father has promised; but stay in the city until you have been clothed with power from on high" (v. 49). The promise of the Holy Spirit was given to each apostle in the form of "tongues of fire" (Acts 2:3) and, subsequently, to each and every Christian, down to the present age, in the form of the indwelling Spirit Himself (see Acts 2:38). We are strengthened with power by the Holy Spirit (see Ephesians 3:16). The gospel came to us with the Holy Spirit and with power (see 1 Thessalonians 1:5).

A church that relegates the Holy Spirit to the first century relinquishes any claim to power in the twentieth century. Unfortunately, if the Holy Spirit were to suddenly die (and of course, such a thing is completely impossible), most of our churches would go on with business as usual. A church that does not live in the power of the Spirit cannot make a claim to being the New Testament Church.

We need to restore the biblical doctrine of the Holy Spirit. Bethlehem is God with us. Calvary is God for us. Pentecost is God in us. The Bible says the Spirit gives us life (see 2 Corinthians 3:6). The reason many of our churches today are dead is because they have not availed themselves of the Holy Spirit.

A few years ago one of our missionary families from South Africa returned to the United States on furlough. They stayed in the home of one of our elders. One afternoon their three-year-old daughter, with pen in hand, was making some remarkable scribbles on a piece of paper. The elder's wife, noticing her work of art, asked her, "What is that?"

Linda replied in a splendid South African accent, "I'm writing a letter."

The elder's wife then asked, "What does it say?"

Linda wasted no time on that one: "I don't know! I can write, but I can't read."

Her response reminds me of much of the yellow journalism I've read in some religious journals in recent years. While we don't have a geographical headquarters, different segments of our churches have certainly had their editorial headquarters. I firmly believe that a

---

A CHURCH THAT RELEGATES THE HOLY SPIRIT TO THE FIRST CENTURY RELINQUISHES ANY CLAIM TO POWER IN THE TWENTIETH CENTURY.

---

number of our brotherhood writers need to learn how to read the Bible before they write up the brethren.

The sad truth is that for a number of years now we have had to sustain life in many of our churches by keeping various brotherhood issues alive. God's word teaches us that life and power come from the Spirit, not from the issues! Church leaders need to wake up to the fact that wolves are among the flock.

Sociologists warn us that social movements make their way through three distinct stages: a man, a movement, a monument. The last stage may be characterized as a feeding frenzy of sharks so hungry for blood that they eventually even devour themselves.

In the final days before the church was born, the resurrected Christ heartened His disciples by promising them a source of power that would last them until His second Advent. That power was to come from the Holy Spirit. The subject we are dealing with is so important that if unresolved, it will be unsurvivable.

CONFIRMED BY A PRESENCE

The resurrection of Jesus Christ is the most radical event in world history. All the wonderful stories of His life that we have examined thus far in this book would mean little or nothing if it were not for His resurrection.

Not long ago, I was on a flight to Mexico City, listening to a cassette tape by Dr. Anthony Campolo. As the tape played, I began to really get caught up in what he was saying. Dr. Campolo is a renowned sociologist and minister who was speaking on the anthropological principle of totemism. Somehow his sociology and anthropology were all merging into some tremendous theology, and by that time my mind was soaring. Our jetliner may have been cruising somewhere around 33,000 feet, but I assure you that, at least mentally, I was considerably higher than that.

"It's Friday," Campolo said. "Jesus is on the cross. Dead. Gone. No more. That's Friday, but Sunday's coming. It's Friday. Mary's crying her eyes out. Disciples are running in every direction like sheep without a shepherd. No hope in the world. That's Friday, but Sunday's coming. It's Friday. Pilate's washing his hands. Pharisees are calling the shots. Roman soldiers are strutting around with spears. But that's Friday, Sunday's coming. It's Friday and those forces that make people suffer and cry and leave them hopeless and in despair, those forces are in control, but that's because it's Friday, but Sunday's coming. It's Friday and Satan is dancing a little jig and he thinks he rules the world and all the institutions are at his command. Governments do his bidding, businesses do

147

his work. But that's because it's Friday, Sunday's coming."

And then in a very dramatic conclusion, Campolo shouts out at the top of his lungs, "It's Friday!" and on the tape you can hear his audience shout back, "But Sunday's coming!"

If there's anything the church needs today it's some good old-fashioned excitement about the resurrection. In one way of looking at it, when you consider the state of the church and the state of the world, it does seem like black Friday, we just can't wait until Sunday.

But there's also another way to look at it. There's no reason why resurrection Sunday can't be here for us everyday. Sunday's purpose is still here; we are still called to evangelize. Sunday's power is still here; the Holy Spirit hasn't left. And Sunday's person is here; there's an empty tomb in Jerusalem to prove it.

All this was to begin at Jerusalem. But it was never meant to end there. May God bless us as we struggle to recapture the dream.

May God bless us, as we
Watch the Lamb.

THINK TIME

1. What are the first thoughts that come to your mind when you hear the word *resurrection*?
2. What do you feel may be your purpose in the Lord's work?
3. Discuss the Zeitgeist of today's world. How can Christ use us to penetrate it?

4. What does it mean to be clothed with power? Are you?
5. How do you associate with the death and resurrection of Jesus Christ?

[1]Soren Kierkegaard, Journals and Papers (Indiana University Press, Volume II, Entry 2157, and Volume V, Entry 6008).